Right NOW!

"What a fantastic, straightforward, and honest book. I'll be recommending it to all my colleagues."

—**Robert Coorey**, MBA, best-selling marketing author of *Feed A Starving Crowd*

"WOW!—This is the book that I wish I had ten years ago. This book should be mandatory reading for every college student, freelancer, entrepreneur, or anyone looking for a powerful breakthrough in their life and business. Brett has walked the walk when it comes to realizing that life is not only short but precious, and using every moment to make a difference. This fantastic book can be your transformational manual . . . but only if you read it. RIGHT NOW."

—**Aaron N. Fletcher**, business coach and author of *Stand Out: A Simple and Effective Online Marketing Plan for Your Small Business*

"When it comes to achievement and success this is a 'street-smart' guide to a bigger, bolder life!"

—**Mel H Abraham**, CPA, CVA, ABV, ASA CSP, #1 best-selling author of *The Entrepreneur's Solution*, and founder of Thoughtpreneur Academy

"It's a shame how many people fail to IGNITE their Entrepreneurial dreams. This book is the SPARK needed to become an Entrepreneur on FIRE!"

—**John Lee Dumas** of EOFire.com and TheFreedomJournal.com

"Brett is a force of nature who will help you become your greater self and make your greatest contribution."

—**Alex Charfen**, Charfen.com

"I can't say enough about Brett and this powerful book. If you want to start building momentum that will lead towards noticeable and meaningful change in your life (regardless of your current situation) there's no better read than *Right Now!*

If you're looking for encouraging yet practical advice to help you turn your dreams into a reality then you need to start reading *Right Now!* . . . *Right Now!*"

—**Jill Stanton**, ScrewtheNinetoFive.com

"This book gets straight to the point and teaches valuable knowledge that everyone should learn, but very few people do. Brett lives this out in his own life and I'm glad he's finally sharing this with others."

—**Chandler Bolt**, Self-PublishingSchool.com

"If you feel like you're in the hamster wheel of life and have no idea what to do or how to get out, *Right Now!* is the perfect companion. Brett has succinctly identified the key steps required to shift your mindset, give you focus, and propel you into action RIGHT NOW!"

—**Michael O'Neal**, host of the Solopreneur Hour Podcast

"'The two most important days of your life are the day you were born and the day you find out why.' —Mark Twain

I feel honored to know Brett, and I'm so excited that he's sharing his life-changing principles with everyone through this magnificent book.

One of the biggest, most important things you can do is to find your purpose in life, yet so many of us never do it. It's too easy to let the tyranny of the mundane get in the way of a more extraordinary life. It's actually quite tragic that we don't do so. But Brett has made it easy to find your purpose—and that alone is so powerful, but then he goes on in practical and great detail on creating your blueprint to living your life of purpose. What I really admire about this is that Brett makes it so easy and so self-evident through his process.

What good is a book if it changes nothing in your life? Well, this one delivers in a big and powerful way. Read it and follow it, and your life will never be the same. Thank you for your work, Brett—you will help so many people with this powerful message!"

—**Chip Franks**, Chief Joe and Bottle Washer, JoeVolunteer.com

"I have known Brett for a few years now, firstly as a fan of his work, then as a friend. Not only has he provided IMMENSE value to my group, but also to me as person. Simply put, Brett has it together! Great wife, great business, great life—If I am going to take advice from anyone, it's going to be a guy like Brett. Whether it's the way he handles the obstacles that life throws at you, his ability to grow a raving group of fans, or change someone's life—I trust Brett to deliver every time."

—**Dan Meredith**, serial entrepreneur, author, speaker, and glorious leader at *Coffee With Dan*

"So many people fail to reach their potential. This book is ideal for anyone who wants to live life at the highest level of greatness. Brett Campbell lives a life of integrity, and he wrote this book to show you how you can do the same. I highly recommend it for anyone who is striving to continuously better themselves."

—**AJ Mihrzad**, best-selling author of *The Mind Body Solution*, OnlineSupercoach.com

"So many people fail to make their dreams a reality because their setbacks feel insurmountable. Reading the tips in this book will help anyone overcome that obstacle and succeed."

—**Anthony Trucks**, B.S., C.S.C.S., and former NFL player

"If you want to quickly discover the simple secrets to success, you need to read Brett's book. It's packed with actionable, practical steps for determining your vision, creating clear steps to gain momentum, and how to feel absolutely unstoppable as you do it! If you're not where you want to be in life—physically, emotionally or financially—it's very likely because you're not applying the strategies inside *Right Now! Why Not You and Why Not Now!*"

—**Justin Devonshire**, international speaker, trainer and leading expert for Coaches, Trainers & Consultants, host of the *Expert Authority Show* on iTunes, justindevonshire.com

"So many people fail to take action in their lives and therefore live a life of mediocrity. Reading the tips in this book will help anyone overcome that obstacle and succeed."

—**Josh Felber**, JoshFelber.com, two-time best-selling author, Emmy Award–winning executive producer, and serial entrepreneur

"Why *not* you, and why not *now*? The first time I heard similar words years ago, they struck a deep cord within me and spurred me to pursue my larger purpose with greater intentionality. However, the gap between 'wanting to' and 'knowing how to' often seemed insurmountable. Brett Campbell's insightful and inspirational book, *Right Now!* provides a detailed road map for traversing the gap and achieving your dreams. With authentic personal stories and anecdotes, Campbell outlines the journey with remarkable clarity, from discovering your unique purpose to useful insights as to what's holding you back. He reveals practical and actionable steps every one of us can take to go from 'wanting to' to 'knowing how to.'"

—**Susie Albert Miller**, MA, MDiv, speaker and coach, author of *Listen, Learn, Love: How to Dramatically Improve Your Relationships in 30 Days or Less!*

"This book gets straight to the point and teaches valuable knowledge that everyone should learn, but very few people do. Brett lives this out in his own life, and I'm glad he's finally sharing this with others.

Right Now! is possibly the most important 'how-to' book if you want to catapult your life to a whole new and exciting level . . . at breakneck speed. Brett has uncovered a super effective and easy-to-use four-step process to almost INSTANTLY tap into your GENIUS and finally live your life to its full potential. Straight off the bat, Brett will have you answering questions that'll automatically trigger your brain into finding CLARITY for your true purpose. But it doesn't stop there . . . You'll also be masterfully guided into designing the frictionless path to achieve all you've ever wanted . . . and more! You won't be able to hold yourself back from implementing this powerful process!"

—**Bret Thomson**, best-selling author, speaker and mentor to thousands on marketing and copywriting, BretThomson.com

"So many people live each day settling for what they believe is all they deserve or can have. If there is one person who has never settled it is Brett. His ability to charge forward on every idea and vision he has, regardless of the risk, has inspired so many people to do the same.

Finally, with this book, for anyone who wants more from their life, Brett has shared the exact steps you need to follow and implement in a simple yet very impactful way. Brett is someone who leads by example and this book is a perfect place to start to learn more about yourself and to strive forward with the confidence you will gain from his teachings."

—**Adam Mckenzie**, author of *POB Me*

Right NOW!

Why not *You*... and why not *Now*?

BRETT CAMPBELL

NEW YORK

NASHVILLE MELBOURNE

Right NOW!
Why not *You*... and why not *Now?*

Published in New York, New York, by Morgan James Publishing. Morgan James and The Entrepreneurial Publisher are trademarks of Morgan James, LLC. www.MorganJamesPublishing.com

The Morgan James Speakers Group can bring authors to your live event. For more information or to book an event visit The Morgan James Speakers Group at www.TheMorganJamesSpeakersGroup.com.

Shelfie

A free eBook edition is available with the purchase of this print book.

CLEARLY PRINT YOUR NAME ABOVE IN UPPER CASE

Instructions to claim your free eBook edition:
1. Download the Shelfie app for Android or iOS
2. Write your name in **UPPER CASE** above
3. Use the Shelfie app to submit a photo
4. Download your eBook to any device

ISBN 978-1-63047-911-4 paperback
ISBN 978-1-63047-913-8 eBook
ISBN 978-1-63047-912-1 hardcover
Library of Congress Control Number: 2015920586

Cover Design by:
Chris Treccani
www.3dogdesign.net

Interior Design by:
Bonnie Bushman
The Whole Caboodle Graphic Design

In an effort to support local communities, raise awareness and funds, Morgan James Publishing donates a percentage of all book sales for the life of each book to Habitat for Humanity Peninsula and Greater Williamsburg.

Get involved today! Visit
www.MorganJamesBuilds.com

Dedication

To my friend Asri Parkinson, who lost her struggle with cancer too soon. Your passing, and the spirit with which you lived your life, showed me that life is too short to not be living to your full potential and started me on this journey. I'll be forever grateful for that gift you gave me. And I won't let you down.

And to my beautiful wife, Emily, whose strength and grace inspire me to be a better man. This book would not be possible without your love and support.

Table of Contents

xii | Right NOW!

Foreword

It's impossible to overlook the extent to which we are impacted by the extraordinary people and relationships that come into our lives, especially if one of those relationships is with someone like Brett Campbell.

I had the makings of a true success story . . . at least on the outside. As the president of two seafood companies, the founder of a thriving international mastermind group, a sought-after speaker in the areas of customer engagement and sales development, a loving husband and proud father of four awesome children, I would have seemed to have it all. People thought of me as a mentor, trusted advisor, and friend. My family loved me unconditionally. I had friends from all walks of life, and we were each other's biggest fans.

On the inside, however, there was a deep, dark hole . . . an inner voice that chastised me on a daily basis for squandering my potential. I was shortchanging myself and I knew it. I was sick on the inside . . . in a very dark place.

Were finances an issue? Sure. This was a struggle due to some overextending in my twenties and thirties.

Was health an issue? You bet. I have seen my weight go from 245 pounds on my wedding day when I was twenty-four years old to over 370 pounds by the time I was thirty-five, and back down to the high 200s where it sits now.

There was always something missing.

I knew I was making a positive impact in the lives of people I came across, but I also knew my impact was just a drop in the bucket. On top of that, the drops were beginning to wear on me, kind of like Chinese water torture. I was tired. I had world-class relationships with dozens of extraordinary people, but my relationship with myself was dysfunctional and destructive.

And then Brett Campbell entered my world.

At first I only knew Brett as an entrepreneurial wizard who lived a life of success, freedom, and constant growth. Brett was known in many circles as a Facebook guru and fitness entrepreneur. I was interested in those topics, so I asked him to speak to my mastermind group, which is called "The Thursday Night Boardroom." Right from the start, I saw there was much more to Brett than entrepreneurial success . . . much, much more.

Brett also has three very firm rules about how he relates to people that immediately connected with me. First, he is not going to tell you what you want to hear if it's not the truth. Second, he won't let you stand in your own way or make excuses about your lack of progress. Third, he won't let you beat yourself up about your lack of progress to the point that it stops you from achieving your goals. He expects you to take consistent action and empowers you to do so.

Brett and I quickly became friends. Even though he lived in Australia and I lived in Southern California, we had an immediate and deep connection. We shared a lot of traits in common, including a sensitive BS meter, a fun-loving sense of humor, a level of candor and vulnerability that seems to draw people close to us, and a strong desire to help people find their superpower.

But Brett has something more, something that is more mindset than learned skill. It is two things, actually. The first is Brett has an innate sense about people. Brett is able to see more in people than they see in themselves and helps them find it themselves. The second is Brett is a teacher at heart and master of strategy. Once he helps people see their true potential and discover their true purpose, he masterfully helps them achieve a richer and more fulfilled life.

Brett has spent his entire life figuring out what to do and then putting frameworks in place to achieve his goals with a focus on setting up processes that make continued success and achievement simple, like being on autopilot.

Brett is a gift and I am honored to be one of the many recipients of his generosity and talents. Brett is an awesome guy to have in your corner. He is a friend, mentor, and advisor, who I can call to discuss *anything* and know I am going to get his empathy, unfiltered feedback, and world-class advice and support.

One of Brett's best qualities is he is always engaged and prepared to help. For example, it has been a couple of years since I had Brett on a call with my Thursday Night Boardroom mastermind. Throughout that time, we grew closer with each other and ultimately started a podcast together, called the "Deep Dive," where we discuss a myriad of topics including marketing, sales strategy, customer engagement, and personal development. The Deep Dive podcast is gold. We share our best strategies and tactics to help people succeed. But while the end product is gold, the off-air, pre-show discussions are magic. Many listeners don't know this, but 80 percent of our episodes start from Brett and me masterminding off air and pressing the record button when we get to something really powerful that we want to share.

During one of our pre-show talks Brett shared he was planning a trip to the United States. I wasn't expecting him to be visiting, and there was something in his voice—a tone—I hadn't heard before from Brett. He sounded more serious than usual, more reserved. I didn't press Brett on that call. His tone made me think it might be better to speak with him in person, so I invited him to stay with me while he was in Southern California, which he did.

One day at lunch Brett and I starting talked about his true purpose for his trip to the U.S. Although he organized the trip around a couple of conferences he wanted to attend, the purpose of the trip was much greater than some keynotes and stale sandwiches. He had just endured a traumatic event that caused him to refocus and adjust the trajectory of his life, and his trip to the United States was a pilgrimage of sorts. He had made a resolution to live a life true to his highest purpose and help others do the same. He determined to never again wait to do the right thing. He resolved to immediately take the first step and the next step, to keep moving in the direction of his heart. He committed to using that traumatic experience to make a meaningful change in his and other people's lives, right away. "Tomorrow is too late," he said. "The greatest contributions we make happen as a result of big decisions followed by small steps in the right direction taken right away."

This system is a product of that revelation. This system will have an enormous impact on who you are and who you'll become. Brett believes your best life is just a group of small steps away from where you are. All you need to know is where you are now, where you are going, a strategy for getting there, and your own resolve.

Brett is the main reason I now have a growing consulting and coaching business. He is also a voice of encouragement that keeps me on track to a healthier and more fulfilled life. If not for Brett's unique brand of encouragement, I'd still be talking about the business and life

I wanted. Instead, I am talking about the business *I have* and the life *I'm living*.

I am excited for you to get started with this book, but I am even more excited for you to finish this book and realize your better, more fulfilled and higher self. When I first met Brett, I think most anyone would have considered my business successful. My company was grossing over $30 million and profitable. But my heart wanted something different, something more. Brett helped me listen to my heart and change direction fast. Within the first week of listening to Brett and following the plan he helped me put together, I landed my biggest client yet. My success since fully adopting Brett's advice has only continued to grow since then.

You're about to embark on a wonderful journey of intrigue, scary moments, desire, and victory—a journey I have been on since meeting Brett. I am honored to have been a part of Brett's journey to an even greater impact on the world and enormously excited to know you'll join us in victory.

Fasten your seatbelt. This is going to be an awesome ride.

To your abundant future,
Jeff Moore
International Pacific Seafoods
Thursday Night Boardroom
jeff@boardroomconsultinggroup.com

Preface

"The greater danger for most of us lies not in setting our aim too high and falling short; but in setting our aim too low, and achieving our mark."
—Michelangelo

You have greatness within you just as you are – *Right Now*.
And you have the ability to activate this unstoppable power – *Right Now*.
I am here to provide you with the instructions for how to make it happen – *Right Now*.
—Brett Campbell

Acknowledgments

I feel so humbled and deeply grateful for the opportunity to put my words to paper and to share a message I feel so strongly about.

This book is dedicated to my friend Asri Parkinson. We lost you too soon. I'll be forever grateful for the gift you gave me throughout this process.

Thank you, Mom. You somehow put up with me and allowed me to be myself, the loud and crazy kid. For doing your best with the cards we were dealt. You made sure we never went without and always put us first. For this I will ensure you will always be taken care of. It's my turn now.

Peter, words can't express how I feel about you and what you have provided for our family. You will always be known as my real Dad.

To my light. Emily, you always believe in me, and always encourage me to be the best I can be. You have taught me how to become a true man and showed me what love truly means.

xx | Right NOW!

Shauna and Kieran, I am so happy to be able to have you be a part of this journey. Everything I do, I do for our family.

Jeff Moore, you were at the starting gates with me on this. Our conversations and your unwavering advice have been nothing short of priceless and something that I will always be so grateful for. Aaron Fletcher, our lunch that day in Encinitas with Jeff was a turning point, and I thank you for being a part of the discovery process.

Nick Pavlidis, you have been instrumental throughout this entire process. Your ability to help capture the true essence of this book has been amazing. Your dedication and effort is something that has my highest admiration.

Karen Anderson, I sought you out for a reason. My dear friend, you have a beautiful soul and such a kind caring nature, I just knew having you be a part of this project would make it the success that it is.

One of my first mentors and now best friend, Jason Urbanowicz, thank you. Your tough love when it counted the most is what kept me on this path and has helped immensely in turning me into the man I am today.

To my two amigos, Daara and Nigel. We've had too many fun times to count. Whilst we now live apart, your friendship is always felt and we'll forever be lifelong friends.

Thank you Morgan James Publishing for picking me out of over 5,000 applications. I am proud to represent such a reputable company whose mission is in line with this entire book. My special thanks to David Hancock, Tiffany Gibson, Alison Garrett, and the rest of the team at Morgan James. This will be our first of many.

Thanks to Adam Mckenzie. What started with simply playing golf led into our very own psychotherapy sessions. Our conversations have been priceless and helpful in ways I cannot express enough.

There have been numerous people who have inspired me along the way: Tony Robbins, Brendon Burchard, Eric Thomas, Les Brown, just to name a few. Your direct and indirect teachings have been profound in my progression.

Joe Polish and Dean Jackson, your *I Love Marketing* podcast was the first real awakening to this amazing world of marketing and Online Business, a vehicle I knew I wanted to be a part of. You have created a monster.

Keith and Kim Brown, your unwavering support and belief in me and my coaching ever since we met have been heartfelt and deeply touching.

To the many amazing people who have worked with me and have trusted my advice, thank you. I am so grateful and fortunate to have worked with you and to have played a small part in your journey. In particular, thanks to my Authority Academy members. I love working with you and helping you shape your dreams and turn them into a lucrative business and life.

My thanks to my amazing friends and colleagues who supported this book: John Lee Dumas, Robert Coorey, Aaron Fletcher, Mel Abraham, Alex Charfen, Michael O'Neal, Chip Franks, Dan Meredith, AJ Mihrzad, Anthony Trucks, Justin Devonshire, Susie Miller, Josh Felber, Chandler Bolt, Bret Thomson, Jill Stanton. You are all power players who are already making such a major impact in this world. I am so privileged to be working alongside you in trying to make this world a better place.

To the 17,000+ Fiit Chick community members and the millions who in some way see our messages weekly, I am proud and privileged to be a part of your journey in any way, shape, or form. You provide the basis for me to be able to do what I do and share what I share. I will be forever grateful.

Finally, as strange as it may sound, my thanks to the teachers who were behind getting me kicked out of school. The reality is that leaving school was probably the best thing that happened to me. It sped up the process and didn't allow me to waste another year trying to figure myself out. It propelled me into action and that may, in fact, have been the biggest gift of all.

Introduction

I never thought it would be possible to live the life I'm currently living and can't express enough gratitude that you're reading this book.

You see, I grew up in a broken home. I was kicked out of high school and worked as a cabinetmaker for five years. I had no "connections," no "network," no natural "opportunities."

As a young child, I dreamed of taking care of my single mother and making sure she would never have to worry about paying the bills or providing for my sister and me. I had no idea how I was going to make it happen, I just knew I had to do it.

I wanted to have the freedom to decide when, where, and how much I worked. I wanted to control how much money I made. I felt trapped in someone else's dream by working for someone else.

I wanted a life where I could wake up every morning and do what I love, and with people I love, every single day.

WOW! Imagine that type of life!

After years of hard work and planning, that life is now my reality.

I am currently sitting in my poolside lounger with my two pet pugs sitting beside me. The sun is shining; my beautiful wife is singing to music like nobody can hear her! The birds are chirping, and I am overcome with happiness and pride.

I own a business that can be operated from anywhere around the world from a simple Wi-Fi connection.

I met and married the woman of my dreams. And I know with certainty that my mother will always be taken care of.

I teach the system I used to create my ideal life—the exact system I share with you in this book—to thousands of others, helping them build momentum towards living their ideal lives, too.

It doesn't get better than that.

The first time I created and implemented this system in my life, amazing things happened. In the first year, I took 174 days off of work, made more money than any previous year in my life, and grew my relationship capital exponentially.

While those outcomes are pretty awesome in and of themselves, the best thing about that year was I was finally living a life *of my own design*. You don't get 174 days off by accident (and keep your job at least). And you certainly don't earn more money than ever before by mistake. I felt happier than ever. I was finally living life on my terms.

I played golf every Monday and Friday. I stopped work at noon no matter what was happening. I had a list of non-negotiables that were actually not negotiable.

You'll see all of the actions, mindset, and physiological strategies that helped me achieve my ideal life and helped thousands of others build momentum towards living their ideal lives, too. Here's exactly how I did it in a simple, but powerful process.

I've studied, applied, taught, and revised this system over time, as I shared it with more people and experienced it in my own life. I may have gotten kicked out of high school, but I became a student of life, learned to teach, taught in order to learn even more, and shared my story to help direct others and inspire them from within. Teaching and sharing this system with others has had an incredible impact on me, personally, because nothing cements a topic in your head like sharing and teaching others.

Some of this system may sound like common sense, and that's okay because it is designed to be something anybody can take even one or two parts from and put into action to improve or redirect their lives. If you find something that you think is common sense, ask yourself whether you are making that common sense your common *practice*. If not, maybe it's time to put that common sense to good use!

I call the system I created the *Right Now* framework because it is designed to help you start building momentum right away. It's unique, created just for you and me. It is filled with exercises, ideas, and a bunch of "how-tos" that you can start using *Right Now*.

You may find some parts that make you stop reading the book and immediately take action. That's great! Many of my clients do. Bookmark your spot in the book and start living your ideal life now—that's what it's designed to do! Other parts will require a little more dedication and time, and that's okay too. The important part is that you start building momentum, immediately.

Sadly, if you can't commit to applying the parts of the system that connect to you, then your life will likely remain the same.

But . . . if you want to experience rapid and exponential improvements in any area of your life, stick with me. Pick out the parts of my system that resonate with you, or put the entire system into action! Let this book be the launchpad for something great in your life. Share it with others. Teach friends or family some of the concepts that resonate with you the most, so you can cement those concepts in your brain and encourage your friends or family to begin building positive momentum in their lives, too.

Developing the "Right Now mindset" can be the catalyst that challenges others to take positive steps towards living their ideal life. By learning to teach, teaching to know, knowing to share, and sharing to inspire from within, you by example, can influence people's hearts and minds and create the life you've always dreamed of.

You can do it. It's your time to shine. You deserve it as much as anyone.

Let's do this!

CHAPTER 1

The Power, the Warning, and the Promise

The Power

How would you like an instruction manual for designing your ideal life?

What you hold in your hands may look and feel like a book, but it's deeper than that. Beyond the words is a carefully crafted plan that's laser-focused on helping you take control of your story, plan your best life, and take action towards achieving your vision of your success. Life is far too short to let your dreams sit idle or to hold yourself back from blossoming into your true and authentic self.

You now hold the ticket to the most important movie on Earth. It's the type of movie that, once you fully engage and allow yourself to be open to the discoveries that lie within, will part the clouds and allow a bright ray of light to guide you onto your path to true purpose. If you haven't guessed it already, the movie I am talking about is about you creating your ideal life!

This movie is much different than any you've ever seen. It's written by you, and for you. You're the writer, lead actor, and director. *You* hold all the power, all the control. And you get all the benefits. The only limitations are the ones you allow to creep into your mind.

As the writer, you determine what you want your ideal life to look like, and most importantly what you achieve by the end. You develop the big vision of your best future. As the lead actor, you're the star of the show, get to take all the steps along the way to achieving your goals, and add your personal touch as your story evolves. As the director, you oversee turning your script into something beautiful and inspiring. You direct any small or big adjustments to make sure your movie has a meaningful ending.

You're in charge. You get to decide what your movie will look like. And your actions as writer, lead actor, and director will determine whether your story is a box office success or a straight-to-DVD flop. Production starts *Right Now*.

Right now is the time to start taking control, planning your ideal life and committing to moving forward as the best version of yourself.

This book is your instruction manual to do so. The following pages outline a step-by-step process to walk you through exactly what you must do to achieve this level of preeminence. I give you practical and very manageable steps to start building momentum—*Right Now*—no matter where you are. I also give you exercises to use and implement immediately to gain massive traction in a short period of time. And I share examples from my own life and the lives of others who have worked through this same process, about overcoming mental, physical, health, and societal challenges to dream again, and then make those dreams a reality.

The Warning

This process is powerful.

I must warn you. This process is not for everyone. It's not for anyone looking for an easy fix or for someone else to solve all their problems. But it's for anyone seeking a greater quality of life and an opportunity to become his or her true and authentic self. It's for anyone seeking to perform at their best. It's for anyone who finds themselves continually asking "Now what?" or who knows there's a better life out there and just needs a little guidance.

The principles outlined in the pages that follow can help you enhance your relationships, improve your habits, help more people, make more money, improve your health, live a life of purpose, and truly make a difference and contributions to the world in ways that matter to you. If you're looking to do any of that, then this is for you.

In fact, as Anna, a recent attendee at one of my events where I taught the *Right Now* process, told me this process is "life changing." She explained: "It opened my eyes up to things I didn't even realize about my own life. The main thing I implemented was changing how I viewed everything in my life and taking a positive role, particularly when things come up that I knew might not go my way. I have improved my results and everyone can see how much brighter I am."

That brings me to one more important point: This is a safe place for you to dream, plan, and implement. In fact, I encourage it!

Your dreams are just as important as anyone else's. If you want to backpack across the world, living off of the land, your dream is just as important as someone who wants to grow a billion-dollar business.

It doesn't matter if you've read enough books and attended enough self-help seminars to sink a battleship, or if you are new to discovering the power of having a set process to design your ideal life. And it doesn't matter if you're a high-level CEO, a stay-at-home mother, or a dog walker.

We all have different challenges and opportunities, ups and downs, setbacks and breakthroughs. Some people's challenges may be different, more extreme, or more frequent, than others, but we all have challenges. And our opportunities might fluctuate as we go through different seasons of life, but we all have opportunities.

A single mother of three certainly has different challenges and time constraints than a twenty-something college student on a full scholarship. Young couples with newborn twins have different challenges and time constraints than empty-nester retirees. And those who have temporary or permanent physical limitations have different challenges and time constraints than those who are not limited.

While those with fewer challenges may find themselves able to move faster, everyone can start moving in the direction of achieving their dreams—*Right Now*. So whether you're closing multimillion-dollar deals on a daily basis, elbows deep in dirty diapers, or saddled with credit card debt, this can help you. That's the beauty of it and what makes it different than any "seven steps to freedom" plan you've come across.

Wherever you are, whatever season of life you're in, and whatever challenges you face, you can design and implement a plan to start moving—*Right Now*—in the direction of achieving your dreams. Your status level has no credit here. Your bank account is irrelevant. Your paycheck doesn't matter. If you're looking to improve your life and the world around you, then you, my friend, are about to embark on the journey of a lifetime.

The Promise

You have inside you what it takes to start designing, and living, your best life—*Right Now*!

Throughout these pages I'll challenge you to ask yourself some tough questions. Those questions, if you fully commit to digging deep to find your true answers, will provide insight into thoughts, feelings, and desires you never knew existed. Your life will never be the same. I know that's a big statement, but it's true.

In fact, you don't even need to implement every last word of this process to make a meaningful positive impact on your life. You can be well on your way to building the life you want—and deserve—by implementing even 20 percent of it. Implement the parts you recognize will benefit you the most.

As you're reading, you'll identify with some of my stories and examples, so strongly that you may think I've been reading your mail. (I promise I haven't!) But I *have* been where a lot of you are *Right Now*. And I have helped others who have been where others of you are *Right Now*. I know the struggles. I've felt the doubt. I've fallen down, and I've felt hopeless. But I also know what it's like to be on the other side of the struggle—to fight through and succeed. And I know you can do it, too.

You may not agree with everything I say. In fact, you might outright oppose some of it. And that's fine. I respect you and your opinions. All I ask is you don't let a small difference in opinion distract you from many powerful lessons and hidden gems that are awaiting you, because those lessons and gems can help you start moving towards living a *life of true purpose*.

Because of that, I suggest you identify the exercises that resonate with you the most, the ones that feel almost too close to home, and start there. You'll be able to immediately plug these strategies and discoveries into your life and start seeing results right away.

Finally, you can also expect me to cut through the crap and tell it like it is. Although I try to be caring, compassionate, and energetic, I won't let you cheat yourself out of designing and building your ideal life by holding back the truth. I want you to succeed. I know you can, no matter how challenging things may feel *Right Now*.

I won't let you cheat yourself out of success.

CHAPTER 2

How to Start Building Your Best Life

H ave you ever had the feeling that there has to be more to life, that there's something better you're supposed to be doing? Do you ever feel that you *know* there's a bigger purpose for you on this planet? If either of the answers to those questions is "yes," you're not alone.

Well I'm not normally a statistics guy, but I found it interesting that every year, Harris Poll® surveys U.S. adults to identify what percentage of them are happy, and, every year, they find only about one-third of them are. On top of that, although factors like gender, relationships, spiritual beliefs, income, expectations concerning future income, and age all had a *marginal* effect on happiness, no single factor caused happiness to be observed in more than 42 percent of respondents.

Imagine that. Out of all of the factors measured, they couldn't find anything that caused more than 42 percent of U.S. adults to be happy. How could so many people be unhappy? What keeps them from doing something to increase their happiness? Why wouldn't they do something, *Right Now*, to improve their lives?

On the other end of the spectrum, what makes the third of adults who are truly happy different? What makes *them* happy, and why *them*? Why not *you*, and why not *now*?

I have committed the better part of my adult life to analyzing those questions.

I started working in my late teens and early twenties, spending five years as a cabinetmaker and becoming one of the best in the area. I was extremely successful in my field, yet I was unhappy.

After five years, I took a leap, taking out thousands of dollars in student loans to go to college and pursue a career in the fitness industry, another interest of mine at the time. Within the first year, although I had confirmed my love for fitness and helping others improve their lives through improving their health, I realized college was not for me. Once again, I took a leap, dropping out of college and pursuing another way to enter the fitness industry.

In a matter of months I earned a different fitness-industry certification and then spent the next couple of years building one of the most expansive and fastest-growing health and fitness brands in Australia, focusing on educating and motivating women to live a healthy, active, fulfilled life. This was one of the first times I felt connected to a larger purpose. That feeling helped keep me going and growing, and, now, the company's messages reach over five million people each week.

As I helped more and more women get healthy, I began to realize I was changing too. For the first time in a long time I felt alive. At that point I knew I was starting to discover my true purpose for being on this planet. It was just the tip of the iceberg, I would later discover, but by that time I was hooked.

I was determined to discover the key to true happiness and personal fulfillment, and to then develop a way for me to help more people. I knew from my work in the fitness industry that whatever I developed needed to be simple, flexible, and customizable, so it could fit the particular needs of each individual using the system.

I began interviewing and surveying people about what made them happy and where they needed improvement. In surveying over 4,500 participants, I discovered careers were one area where people struggled the most, with more than half of them either unhappy with their job or career path or completely *hating* what they were doing for a living. I also discovered that objective personal or professional success had no relation to overall happiness, as those who were objectively successful in business or other aspects of life had the same level of dissatisfaction as those who lacked objective success indicators.

I also studied what made people start, push through adversity, and ultimately achieve their goals. In addition to analyzing the best business leaders in the world, clients of my fitness business, and friends and family, I looked inward at what had helped me achieve goals from a young age, including what helped me successfully shift gears from cabinetmaker, to college student, to fitness professional, and ultimately to building one of the fastest-growing fitness brands in Australia before my thirtieth birthday.

The more I researched, and the more I self-examined, the clearer the critical distinction became: those who were truly fulfilled were living a life congruent with their true purpose in life. They were successfully doing something that truly mattered to them.

That explained why I was so unhappy as a cabinetmaker and student compared to how fulfilled I felt helping people improve their lives by improving their health. It also explains why so many people are unhappy in life, working jobs they took because it was the next natural step after their education or because one of their parents believed it was a good career track.

Based on that information, I started focusing on helping people discover what their true purpose in life was so they could start making changes that were meaningful to them. I also continued my own personal shift from helping people improve their health and fitness, to helping people improve their lives and satisfaction as a whole.

As I began working with more and more people, I discovered what separated those who started and then continued to build momentum towards living a life of their dreams from those who did not. Both groups saw the *big* change they wanted to make in their lives, however the group who successfully took action broke that big change down into little steps they could start taking right away. They had developed a plan full of small steps they believed were achievable. The other group, on the other hand, saw the big change as one giant leap and froze.

Gathering more information, I developed and refined a system that was both powerful and customizable, helping friends, family, and clients get unstuck and get on paths towards designing and living their dream lives. I began speaking and leading workshops to help groups and individuals learn the system and how to apply it to their lives so they could discover and reach their true purpose in life.

This system began changing lives. A single mother who struggled with her weight the majority of her adult life, who had bills piling up around her, and who ultimately felt hopeless, started making positive changes to her health she once thought were impossible. A businessman who was frozen with doubt and struggling with transitions, cleared his mind, rediscovered his passion for his work, and saw for the first time how his business helped him fulfill his greater purpose. And countless entrepreneurs who knew they were destined for more, but did not know where to start or who to turn to, found the clarity, direction, and support to confidently move forward building businesses that matter.

One by one, clients, friends, and family members were building momentum towards living a life that mattered to them, achieving levels of happiness and purpose they once thought impossible. The power of this system was electrifying. Thousands of people went from thinking "I can't" to "Why not me?" from "Not now" to "Why not now?"

As I continued to help more people, my own life continued to shift. It was a gradual shift at first, because I had felt relatively content with my career in the fitness industry. I was helping people make meaningful changes in their lives and enjoyed doing it. Although I felt even happier as I helped people make bigger changes in their lives, I was generally happy right where I was.

That all changed, however, in a two-week period during which a terrible tragedy caused me to change the way I viewed my life and the time we have on this planet.

A dear friend of mine, Asri, was only twenty-five years old when she was diagnosed with breast cancer. She underwent treatment and we were all relieved when she was told she beat it.

It was only a few years later when she got a headache that was different than a usual headache. It was so severe she decided to go to the doctor to get it checked out. Sensing her pain was unusual, her doctor suggested they perform a few scans "just as a precaution" to make sure everything was normal.

But everything was far from normal. The scans revealed Asri had developed a large brain tumor and it was growing rapidly. As young, strong, and determined as Asri was, this time around it was going to be even harder to beat.

Asri was tenacious and gave it everything she had. She went through multiple rounds of treatment and was committed to doing whatever she could to beat cancer for the second time. As the months went on, she made great strides, and once again, we grew optimistic. After several rounds of therapy, Asri was doing well.

One night, I got this overwhelming sense I should call Asri's husband, Daara, to see how she was doing. Daara was his usual, optimistic self as he relayed the progress she had made. Asri had finished her last round of therapy and was home.

But my intuition kept trying to tell me something. I kept feeling like I should plan a trip to see Asri in person. I asked Daara when he thought might be a good time to come visit. "Whenever you want, really," Daara assured me. "It's totally up to you since she's so much better."

We agreed I'd come visit in a couple of weeks.

Never one to procrastinate, I got off the phone and went online and found some flights a few weeks out.

Just as I was about to buy my ticket, another wave came over me. For the second time in an hour, I felt like my intuition was trying to tell me something.

I called Daara back and told him I was changing my plans and coming sooner. He said, "Cool, but, *really*, there's no hurry if you can't come now." But somehow I knew I couldn't wait a couple of weeks. When we hung up I booked a ticket leaving the soonest I could, in four days.

I arrived very late in the evening, so I called Daara to let him know I landed and would be by in the morning. He said Asri was doing well and she had no idea I was coming to visit. He thought the surprise would be good for her.

Early the next morning I took a taxi to their house. As I got out of the taxi, Daara came walking down the driveway towards me.

The look on his face said it all. Something was terribly wrong.

He hugged me and said "Hey, Asri took a bad turn last night. She was up all night with a horrible cough, she was struggling to speak, and she couldn't keep her eyes open for longer than a minute."

We quickly walked towards the house as my heart lodged into my throat. My stomach twisted and my mind raced. "A bad turn" are words you never want to hear in this situation. I didn't know what to say or do. I felt helpless.

We walked through the front door and into their small living room. In the middle of the room there was my dear friend Asri, lying on a hospital bed, her eyes closed. After an all-night battle, she had finally fallen asleep, so I walked over to the bed and quietly sat down beside her. I took her hand and held it. It was so cold.

After a few minutes, she slowly opened her eyes. I knew she had been in a lot of pain, but for just a moment, I could see in her eyes that the pain wasn't her focus. Her eyes were full of joy. She gave me a big smile, the way she always did.

"Hello, beautiful," I said.

"Brett. Thank you for coming," she replied in a croaky, faint voice. She closed her eyes again and drifted back to sleep.

That was the last time we ever spoke.

A few minutes later she woke up coughing, in awful pain. We did everything we could to make her comfortable.

Three hours later, she was gone.

Her funeral was a few days later; the shock still overwhelming. As I was flying home, my mind was flooded with images, the reality of what had just happened finally sunk it. I began pouring back through my life. I questioned almost everything I had thought about myself. I even began questioning whether my "success" in the fitness industry was actually working against me—holding me back from doing something bigger.

I realized in that moment, although I was rising to the top of an industry that helps people live a longer, healthier life, my real passion and purpose was to help people achieve much more than just physical fitness.

I mourned the loss of Asri, one of the sweetest, toughest, most inspirational people on the planet, and wondered where my life was going.

It was then I began to focus with laser-light clarity on the essential areas where I could improve in my life.

It was an epiphany, 30,000 feet in the air. I felt my sense of urgency rise. My satisfaction with where I was in life disintegrated. I couldn't wait any longer to live my larger purpose. I couldn't waste any more time. I couldn't leave my life to chance.

I asked myself these questions: When all is said and done, could I look back and say I had lived a life of intention?

Did I love with passion?

Did I do everything in my power to follow my dreams and never give up?

For years I thought the answers to those questions were easy yeses. I had built a successful health and fitness company from scratch. I made a good living. I had a lot of friends, and I had strong relationships with my loved ones.

Despite all those successes, I didn't feel whole. At first I wasn't sure why. My answers were truthful. But the more I pressed the more I realized I wasn't going deep enough. I realized I hadn't discovered my real answers to those questions. My answers were superficial.

It turns out I was still searching for the true meaning in my life, the meaning that was bigger than any business, and even bigger than myself. I was still searching for deep relationships and clear directions for achieving my ultimate dreams.

I examined myself, what I had accomplished, and the direction in which my life was heading. With a new perspective, my life didn't seem very successful, not in the way I wanted it to be. I was a couple of degrees off, and I knew it. I wasn't living to my highest potential. I just *knew* I could give more to this world, but I had a lot more work to do.

I fought hard to keep the "buts" away. You know the "buts." Those are the little phrases we tell ourselves are reasons why we can't do something or why we need to wait for some other event to happen first before we can take action. These "buts" are sometimes referred to as the stories we tell ourselves that cause us to self-sabotage. If you don't believe you're destined for greatness, that will be your future. You won't do what it takes. On the other hand, if you believe you're meant to achieve greatness, you'll do the work it takes to do so.

The thought popped in my head that I would like to someday become a coach and motivational speaker. But that sounded crazy. "Become a coach and motivational speaker? Me? But I am a fitness guy. I am a businessman. Who wants to hear me speak? Who cares what I have to say?" I thought. So I challenged myself and started asking myself different questions.

Instead of asking *why me?* I asked *why not me?* My dreams were just as valid as anyone else's. Why shouldn't I start becoming the best version of myself?

Instead of *why now?* I asked *why not now?* Not tomorrow, not in a week or a month. Why not start *right now?* Just like the first question, I was no different than most people. Why couldn't I get started pursuing my true self right then and there, right on that plane?

When I really pushed myself I discovered there was *nothing* stopping me from taking steps towards my dreams, but me. I was the one who could make a difference in the direction my life was going. Even in a metal tube flying over 30,000 feet above earth, I was planning, analyzing, and dreaming. Surely I could continue that momentum when the wheels hit the ground.

The impact of realizing the control I had over the direction of my life took me by surprise. In reality, nothing was getting in the way, but me.

If I want to lose weight, I need to eat better and exercise more. If I want to mend relationships, I need to take personal responsibility for acting differently (or apologize about something I should have apologized for long ago). If I want to make more money, I need to work harder or smarter and show I am worth more than I am being paid.

It's really that simple. What I realized is I basically needed to do four things. I needed to discover my true self, design a plan to lead me there, develop the skills and support system to keep me moving in the right direction, and then take action to deliver the best results possible.

Asking and answering these tough questions had me on a whole new path to a better place. I felt the momentum building and knew these same questions could help others feel the same. I knew others, like me, needed to learn how to discover, design, develop, and deliver their best life possible. And I realized we all needed to do it sooner rather than later. I now had my focus, purpose, and direction clear.

My heart broke that day when I lost my dear friend, Asri.

But the plan that began to take shape, right on the plane, is now being used in ways I never expected. Although I saw its bigger potential, I initially designed the plan to only help me discover and then fulfill my true purpose. Since that time, I refined that plan and developed it into a system anyone can use, no matter where they are in life, to discover their true purpose and start taking small, but meaningful steps towards living their ideal life.

Let me tell you about Kim and Adam.

Kim is a wife, mother, and full-time fitness professional. She struggled to grow her business in a way that didn't require more and more of her time. She wanted more clients without having to work so many hours. Using the same concepts and process as in this book, Kim created a manageable plan that focused on high-impact action steps that caused her to start making more money without requiring more and more of her time. Even better than the business success, however, was the effect on Kim, personally. In her words, this process caused her "to look into herself in a more honest way in order to find what was important to her" and "identify values in her life she had never considered." Just like Kim, the concepts and process in this book can help you get past what is holding you back, and focus on high-impact personal and professional progress.

A good friend of mine, Adam, came to me looking for direction. He felt unfulfilled and unsure, but quickly rediscovered his talent and desire to teach others. Within three months of our first conversation, Adam used the *Right Now* framework to write his first book and hold his first live teaching event.

This plan helped Kim, Adam, me, and thousands of others let go of our pasts, take inventory of our presents, and take control of our futures. It can take you from discovering your true purpose in life, to designing your schedule and surroundings to support your new path, to developing yourself and your support in a way that continually moves towards personal fulfillment, and, finally, to delivering the best results possible.

As you learn the system, I want you to remember it's designed to be flexible and customizable. Just like there's *no* one-size-fits-all life, there's *no* one-size-fits-all plan. Different people have different obligations and responsibilities in life, so an effective plan must be flexible enough for anyone to adapt it to their circumstances. For example, no one should expect a single parent to take the same actions as a single student because the parent has more responsibilities and risk. But the parent can still do *something, Right Now*, to start building momentum towards their ideal life. This plan will help them do that. Their steps may be smaller, or more deliberate, but they can still take *some* steps.

I'll push you. I'll challenge you to think and act outside of your comfort zone. For you to make any meaningful impact on your life, the most important thing for you is for you to do *something* to start building momentum, *right now*. I want you to step a little bit out of your comfort zone and challenge yourself. But I also want you to read this while asking yourself how this system can be customized for your particular life situation, so you too can start making meaningful changes to your life and not wait until it's too late.

For me, it took the tragedy of losing a dear friend to a horrible disease to realize I had not been living a life true to my larger purpose. You might not need that level of discomfort to push you in a different direction. Whatever you need, and whatever your purpose is, this system can help. A recent student of mine, Roz, came to me without a specific goal, but rather simply looking to increase confidence, find direction, and stay focused. After working through these exercises and implementing these strategies, Roz identified several fears that were holding her back from a happier and healthier future.

Whatever your motivation, this system can help you identify your strengths, values, and true purpose in life and then take action towards achieving that, because there's no reason you can't start building momentum towards achieving your biggest dreams.

So let me ask you . . .

Why *not* you, and why not *now*?

For the vast majority of people, there's no good reason you can't have what you want, and no good reason you can't start taking steps towards having it all starting *right now*.

CHAPTER 3

The Four Phases of the
Right Now Framework

*"The value of life lies not in the length
of the days but in the way that we use them."*
—Michale Monatigen

Discover, Design, Develop, and Deliver

The *Right Now* framework is simple and involves four phases, from looking inward to taking deliberate action and achieving great success. Because each phase builds upon the previous one, it's important that once you get to Chapter 4, you follow along in order and do not skip ahead, no matter how excited you get!

Phase 1 – Discover
The first phase of the *Right Now* framework is the Discover Phase. This phase is critical because in order to make a meaningful life transition,

you must first identify what you're looking to achieve. Despite its importance, this phase is the most overlooked. Many books, courses, or other content focus so much on "seven steps to success" or "five things to do today to supercharge your life" and skip right over the fact that it doesn't matter how many steps you take if you're heading in the wrong direction. You could have the best plan in the world, but if you're not aiming at a destination of true meaning—to you—then you're not going to end up anywhere worthwhile.

The Discover Phase is also the most challenging. It involves you, a mirror, and the ability to take a good hard look at all areas of your life. It will challenge you to uncover the truth about who you really are and what you really stand for, whether it's a high-powered executive, or a world-class mom, like Letitia, who worked through the *Right Now* framework with me recently and improved her relationships with her kids, along with her self-image, by discovering who she truly was, and asking herself tough questions that revealed that she was already doing a great job raising her kids. Beginning with the Discover Phase, Letitia made incredible shifts in her mindset, eliminated the bottle of wine she used to drink each night, and even stopped taking antidepressant medication (on the advice of her doctor, of course). Letitia now sees that she is worthy, enough, and deserves to be happy and loved. She also is huge inspiration to me and those around her!

By the end of Phase 1, you'll discover these truths, too, and determine where you really want to go so you can design your path to get there.

Phase 2 – Design

In this phase you, will start creating the environment in which you'll set yourself up for success. You'll design your plan of action to get you exactly where you want to go.

Too many people skip over the planning phase and just start randomly doing things they think might generally push them towards their goals. Although that can provide temporary or small benefits, it's crucial to put together a simple, but detailed plan from where you are to where you want to go. If you wanted to build a house, you wouldn't just start nailing wood together because you know houses are made of wood and nails, would you? Of course not. You'd create a plan.

The same is true with your life, and the Design Phase walks you through your personal process for success and helps you make sure your surroundings are pushing you towards your goals (instead of sabotaging your success).

The Design Phase is my answer to the very first question people ask me when they hear I live my life the way I want, play golf two times a week, work an average of three days a week, and take several vacations a year with only a couple of weeks notice.

"How do you do it?" they ask. It's simple. I design my life that way.

I haven't always been able to have that much freedom and flexibility. Heck, there have been times where I would work all-nighters from time to time or work weeks on end with little time off. But I discovered the process to do that and when I decided to take more control of my life, I started designing my life to be built around that freedom and flexibility. The Design Phase can help you do the same.

Phase 3 – Develop

By Phase 3 you'll know where you are, where you're going, and how you'll get there. Pretty incredible, right? Once you have that down you're ready to start developing the personal and relational traits to implement your plan. This phase is one of my favorites because it really connects with my entrepreneurial brain, my creative side, and the doer within me.

In this phase, I walk you through developing the psychology, physiology, personal knowledge, and productivity traits to become the best performing version of yourself, along with how to develop the right support around you.

(Don't worry, I have created a unique and simple framework to guide you through this, along with some incredibly effective how-to tips that will blow your mind! In fact, Leianne, a woman I worked with recently, told me that after implementing several parts of the lessons in the Develop Phase, an old friend remarked how young she looked, her mindset is better than ever, and she has been a great role model for her kids and granddaughter!)

When you're done with Phase 3 you'll have everything you need to start taking action towards living the life of your dreams. The only thing left is Phase 4. (This is where the rubber hits the road.)

Phase 4 – Deliver

By the time you get to Phase 4 you'll be ready to take massive action. That's why this phase is all about "the how-to." In Phase 4, I help you supercharge your success and get the most out of your life. I help you get and stay on track with your plan. As you work through the Deliver Phase you'll begin to see your life coming into shape, just as you designed it.

So strap yourself in, and prepare to embark on the adventure of a lifetime.

Right Now is your time to start, it's your time to draw a line in the sand and step into a new world full of joy, love, and abundance. A world full of hopes and dreams. And a world full of greater contributions that matter to you.

This process is my gift to you as you start walking towards that new world. This is *my* contribution to you becoming the best you can be, to be the *you* that you know is inside you, ready to bust out!

So let me ask you one more time: Why *not* you? And why not *now*?

I am confident that, as you explore the four phases of the *Right Now* framework, you'll agree that there's no good reason you can't live your ideal life and there's no reason you can't start *Right Now*.

Caution: This doesn't mean you should quit your job immediately and travel the world in the name of achieving your dreams (even if you want to because your boss is a jerk), especially if you have responsibilities like mouths to feed or bills to pay. But I *am* simply suggesting you start somewhere and start small. What I *am* suggesting is, if you've been frozen in inaction because you're rightfully dedicated to important responsibilities, you *can* start looking, researching, and investigating other options. You *can* start taking small, momentum-building steps towards achieving your dreams. You *can* start *Right Now*.

But the good news is you'll find this process to be very easy to read and very easy to do. You'll also find practical exercises along the way and some questions to answer, with space right here on the pages to answer them, as I guide you through the four phases of the *Right Now* framework.

It's important that you take the time to do the exercises and answer the questions while the material is fresh in your mind and heart. This process can be your launching pad to something incredible. Taking the time to work through the exercises and answer the questions as the material is fresh is key to becoming a supercharged success like Norm, who attended one of my events recently, implemented the *Right Now* framework right away, and wrote to me that he's seen an influx of clients and has never felt more loved or loving in his personal life.

That's what I'm talking about!

Are *you* ready?

Get your pen, pencil, sticky notes, or whatever else you use to create, and let's get to work.

PHASE 1
DISCOVER

CHAPTER 4

Who Are You, Really?

I was five years old. It was a sunny day and I was playing outside in the yard. Suddenly, I heard a loud scream that sounded like my name. I paused.

There it was again. It *was* my name. And it was my mother's voice screaming out to me from inside my family's motor home. I ran towards her voice, up the steel steps, and shot my head through the open window. My mother was in trouble. My father had just gotten home from another day wasted at the local pub. He was drunk, as usual, and he and my mother were arguing. The argument escalated and he was about to throw her through the window.

My mother screamed "Brett, run and get help!" I cried and ran to a neighbor's as fast as I could.

Help arrived for my mother, and shortly after that horrific day, she took my sister and me and left on a quest for a better life. That was last memory I have of my father.

Although my memory of that day is limited, the impact was much greater.

Even though I was only five years old, I declared to myself I would be the man of the family from then on and take care of my mom and sister. I committed to do whatever it took to make right what my father could—or *would*—not do.

What a massive responsibility for a little boy to put on his shoulders, right? It was, trust me. But in the long run putting that huge weight on my shoulders gave me what I now believe was an unfair advantage. It made me learn to hustle. It helped me discover what it really took to achieve something important and bigger than myself. It helped me learn the true power of never giving up.

Although learned under extreme circumstances by necessity and with a lot of bumps and bruises, those lessons helped me develop deep-rooted qualities that form the foundation for me to achieve my dreams and help others do the same.

Even after that early turmoil, turnaround, and future business successes, I always felt like there was something still missing in my life. I couldn't put my finger on it. I just knew it was there. It didn't matter how hard I hustled, how hard I worked, or how much success I achieved, there was always an empty feeling deep in my soul.

From an early age, my life had been directed by a feeling of a responsibility to succeed, at first for my mother, my sister, and me, and later to help others. But, in doing so, I wasn't able to develop the most meaningful achievement of all: living in my true identity.

By the time I hit my twenties, I was all grown up physically, but I still had no idea who I truly was. I was just a young man looking to find and pursue the next business opportunity. I was moving so fast from opportunity to opportunity that I forgot to pause and figure out what was really important to me.

I'll say that again. For over two decades I was chasing opportunities that were meaningful to other people and that were good. Still, I was building their dreams, not mine. I was transactional, and in being so transactional I had never gotten to know who I truly was and what I was on this planet to do!

So before I walk you through Phase 1 of the *Right Now* framework, let me ask you this:

Do you know who you are, who you *really* are?

What unique gifts are you hiding from the world? I don't want you to be one of those people whose hopes, dreams, and talents are buried with them, six feet under the ground, after a life lived only to a fraction of their potential.

What good could you do in the world if you nurtured and shared your talents?

Phase 1 will help you make sure you can answer those questions with confidence. *Right now.*

The Setup: Asking the Right Questions

"To find the great answers, you must simply ask the great questions."
—Anthony Robbins

When I first heard world-renowned self-help, motivation, and high-performance coach Anthony Robbins say all I needed to do to find great answers was to ask great questions I was taken aback. "What a great concept!" I thought. "But what are the questions?" If you're thinking the same thing, let me shed some light on this for you.

For years, I was a lost young boy walking around in a man's body searching for answers. But I was so caught up in my search for answers that I never stopped to ask myself the right questions. And that was exactly what kept me from finding what I really needed to start living a life of my own design. I had no idea what I was looking for! I was just searching.

It wasn't until I discovered and then asked myself the right questions that I started to find meaningful answers that helped me move in the right direction. Trying to find the answers before you have the right questions is like trying to search for a missing person without knowing what they look like. You can spend a lot of time running around looking busy, but at the end of the day you're no closer to your goal than when you started. In fact, you might have spent all day heading in the wrong direction and be farther away from the missing person than where you started!

But what are the right questions? It took me over a decade to figure that out.

The Search: Finding the Right Questions

My quest for answers started when I was just sixteen years old. It had been eleven years since my mother, sister, and I left that motor home in search of a better life. Although we settled into a new neighborhood soon after that dreadful day, it wasn't the greatest of neighborhoods. Street gangs and poverty were pretty common.

But I managed to avoid most of the negative influences of my surroundings. I was a bit of a talker, with way too much energy, and the attention span of a gnat. But I generally stayed out of trouble. School was a challenge. I wasn't a bad student. I just talked too much in class and some of my teachers said I distracted others. It got to the point that my English teacher put my desk in the hallway to keep me from being a distraction. Every day I'd walk in the classroom, and every day she would point to the door. "There you go, Brett," she would say. "You're out there."

After a while, it apparently took a toll on the administrators because, at sixteen years old, they asked me to leave—for good. I had no idea what to do. I hadn't really thought about life after school at that point, although I knew exactly what would happen when I got home and told my mother. My mother always said I could talk underwater, but this time my mouth had gotten me into deeper water than I could talk myself out of.

Without a plan or any real direction, I did what I thought was best at the time. I took the first job I found that would make my mom happy, keep me off the streets, and have some connection with my talents. I became an apprentice cabinetmaker. I spent five years as a cabinetmaker, which was about four years and 364 days too many. I knew it right away, too. But I felt like my options were limited.

Years later, after losing Asri and questioning nearly everything about my existence, I'm convinced that had I taken a few minutes to explore what I truly wanted in life, or even why I felt my options were limited, I would have left that job much sooner. If I had the courage to allow myself to dream, to ask myself tough questions about who I was and who I wanted to become, I wouldn't have spent five years in a job that drained me, a job that only passed time and paid the bills. I wouldn't have spent five years trading precious time for a mediocre paycheck.

It sometimes pains me to think how little I accepted in the form of a mediocre paycheck for postponing my dreams. That's exactly what it was. I postponed pursuing my dreams in exchange for that job. How much are you being paid to give up on, or even delay, your dreams?

I know the discomfort of asking tough questions that force you to identify the gap between where you are now and where you want to be. I know from the plane that the process is challenging. But I also know that asking and answering those tough questions can be one of the most profound exercises you'll ever do. I know it can give you deeper insights into your wildest dreams and help propel you in a direction *you* choose.

Asking tough questions launched my transition, helped Kim grow her business, and helped Adam rediscover himself and begin teaching others. You may find the exercises uncomfortable at first, but if you hang with me through that discomfort, I *know* you'll find clarity, purpose, direction, and freedom, by the end.

CHAPTER 5

Asking the Tough Questions

In this chapter you'll take the most challenging exercise you'll ever face. It was for me. It was an eye-opener and I have literally never been the same since, in a good way, of course. This exercise will cut you deep, too, but it will help you identify who you really are and where you want to go. Don't worry, I leave you plenty of space to write the answers right on the page. If you prefer, you can write them in your own notebook or journal. But in order to get the most out of this process, writing out your answers to the questions is important.

Here we go.

Imagine it's your funeral. Yes, it's your funeral.

You're lying in the casket, lifeless on the outside, but you can see and hear everything that's happening around you. The funeral services start and one of your closest loved ones walks up to share some words about you and your life. It could be a parent, spouse, son, daughter, brother, sister, uncle, aunt, friend, colleague, community leader, coach, mentor, or spiritual leader.

For the purpose of this exercise, you must choose that loved one. If you're having trouble deciding, just pick the first person who comes to mind when you think of loved ones. Write down their name. This person is going to read your eulogy. But here's the twist: You get to write the eulogy for them—*Right Now*.

The eulogy will cover four key topics (given below), which I'll help you explore. As you're writing, be sure what you are putting down is exactly what you'd want your loved one to be able to honestly say about you. How would you want them to answer the following questions? Go ahead and write your answers here in the book.

1. What type of person were you? Were you happy, joyful, caring, trustworthy, generous, giving, ambitious, etc.? What were the two or three qualities that would describe you best?

2. What principles did you stand for? What causes did you support?

3. What contributions did you make to their life?

4. What will they miss most about you?

It's natural to just list a few points and move on, but I want you to do a little bit more. Once you list the answers to these questions here on the page, take a separate piece of paper and spend fifteen to twenty minutes writing out an actual eulogy based on your answers to those very self-confronting questions.

Like in most exercises, the power and breakthroughs come by actually doing the exercise, and not just by reading the questions. Please do not cheat yourself and keep reading, or say "I want to keep reading so I'll do it later." If you're anything like me you won't! You may have all the intentions to do so, but we both know how that ends. You'll have mentally moved on, so please do yourself a favor and do it now—*Right Now!* Go!

Write as many eulogies as you desire for chosen loved ones to read. I urge you to write at least two, including one to be read by someone with whom you'd like to have an improved relationship. For example, if you're currently going through a bad patch with your spouse, choose them. Going through this exercise with a number of loved ones will help you find clarity faster than you ever thought possible about who you want to be and what you want the totality of your contributions to this world to amount to. I promise you'll start to finally come to grips with who you really are.

I take this exercise in detail at least two times a year with at least five key people in my life. I have written eulogies on behalf of several people from my past and present. One of the hardest ones I ever wrote was on behalf of my father. It's been almost three decades since I last saw him.

Needless to say, the emotions of writing a eulogy to be delivered by him at my funeral told me a lot about who I am and who I want to be.

If you want to read a couple of the eulogies I've written, including ones on behalf of my mother and father, they're available on a page full of resources and extra bonus materials just for people who read this book, which you can find at http://brettcampbell.net/right-now-resources.

Once you're done with your eulogies, move onto the next tough question to help you design your true life.

How Are You Showing Up?

Now that you've completed the exercise and identified the type of person you want to be, you need to check how you're currently showing up in life. Ask yourself are you the person you just wrote about in the eulogy? Are you earning the words you want them to be able to honestly say? Or is the current "you" someone completely different?

If there's a difference between what you'd want them to say about you and what they might realistically say about the person you currently are, that gap gives you incredible insights into changes you may want to take. When I first did this exercise, I had a truly profound moment. I wrote my first eulogy on behalf of my mother. I wrote things like "Brett was a caring and loving boy. He would do anything for me and his sister, and was always there for us at any moment."

When it was time to look at how I was showing up, however, I found a big gap. As much as I thought I was being a caring and loving son, my actions were not consistent with that. I hadn't even talked with my mother in three weeks. What type of caring boy is that? And how was that showing I was always there for her?

My initial reaction was to defend myself. "Well, she hasn't called me either," I rationalized, "so she is as much to blame as me." But that, my friend, is an excuse, not an answer. In fact, that's an exact recipe for disaster because nothing will ever change in a relationship until someone decides to take action, to go first. So instead of defending myself and waiting for her to reach out, I decided to stop playing the blame game and call her.

When she answered I told her about the exercise I had just done, that I wanted our relationship to be better and for us to talk more frequently. We had a great conversation and have been in much more frequent contact ever since. Our relationship is stronger than ever.

This almost immediate win is what makes the *Right Now* framework so powerful. Although not every transformation will be that quick or easy, this very meaningful transformation didn't take months or years. It didn't take days or weeks. It took minutes. Within minutes I had asked myself what I wanted my mother to say about me at my funeral, realized I had not been acting that way, and picked up the phone to start acting more consistent with the eulogy. I told her what I would like our relationship to look like. I let her know my intentions and what I would be doing to live up to the words I wanted her to be able to honestly say at my funeral.

I had just taken personal responsibility for living my life consistent with the impact I want my years here to make, all because I discovered how I was showing up and decided to close the gap between who I was being and how I wanted to be remembered.

This important lesson leads me to the next tough question in the Discover Phase of the *Right Now* framework:

Are You Taking Personal Responsibility for Changing Your Circumstances?

If you want to become healthier, for example, it's up to you to take actions that will make you healthier. You can't blame your partner for buying junk food or your lack of exercise. You're the one who eats the food and you're the one on the couch binge watching reality TV. I hear so many people complain they *can't* eat clean because their partner won't eat what they want to cook. That's a bunch of crap. Sure, it might take more willpower than someone whose partner is a health-food addict. But *can't*? I don't think so. I'm not going to let you get away with that thinking.

If you want better relationships start doing what you can to improve them, just like I did with my mom. Make the first move. Lead by example. Get in that mindset, because the key to making a relationship great is to work at making your relationship great. It's that simple. Great relationships don't just happen. Somebody—in this case you—needs to start making it great.

If you want to achieve anything great, you need to take personal responsibility for the actions you can control to achieve outcomes you desire. That mindset is what allows me to show up as the best-performing version of myself almost all the time. It's like a superpower. Make it your superpower.

CHAPTER 6

Your Purpose Is Waiting for You

L ooking into the past is one of my favorite exercises because it allows you to think without worrying about the challenges of the present or the perceived uncertainty about the future. One of the most frequently asked questions I get is "How do you figure out what your actual purpose in life is, Brett?"

It's one of my favorite questions to get because it tells me two things. First, it tells me the person I am talking with is motivated to make a positive change. I can work with motivated people. Second, it shows me I can have a meaningful impact on their lives with the real answer to the question.

But the truth is, the whole idea of *finding* your purpose is a bit of a misnomer. You don't find your purpose in life. Your purpose finds you. In fact, it already has. Everybody is born with purpose. It's inside you already, hidden somewhere deep within your core. It's ready to come out and flourish and contribute to this world. But you must be ready for it. If you're not ready, your purpose can elude you for years.

Some people are never ready. They close their minds and hearts and never let their purpose find them. The good news is I know you're not one of those people because you've already taken action and invested your time and money to working through the *Right Now* framework.

My purpose found me when I was a young boy, although it was only there briefly before I stopped seeing it because I wasn't open to accepting it at the time. It wasn't until I was sitting on that airplane on my way home from Asri's funeral that it finally dawned on me and I finally saw it again. Unfortunately for me, it took the death of a very close friend for me to come out of my shell and let my purpose find me again, to finally become open, honest, and accepting enough of myself to see it.

Can you see it yet? Don't worry; this exercise will help you see it by having you ask yourself two very powerful questions. These questions will open your mind and heart just wide enough for your true purpose to come out and find you.

It worked for me and it has worked for others. My client Kim, a wife, mother, and entrepreneur, for example, in working through the same principles that you're reading right here, realized she had not been honest with herself for years. When she finally started being honest and open with herself, her confidence and focus skyrocketed. Through answering these questions, she discovered what was most important to her, which was to make sure her personal values were not lost while she worked on growing her business and committed to never give up on that, no matter how hard it seemed at times. With that discovery and focus, Kim reinvigorated her business and made sure it grew in a direction that honored her personal values first and foremost.

When I answered these questions, I finally gave myself permission to live my true purpose. Soon thereafter I was speaking on stages all over the world and helping countless people start living lives of their dreams. Now nothing stops me. Seeing those answers at the beginning of every day tells me what to allow into my life and what to keep out. It shows me what direction I should go next. It helps me become driven from within.

Question #1: If I were to take care of you financially for the rest of your life so you had no more bills and enough money to do whatever you wanted in your life, what would you do with your life and, equally important, what would you no longer be doing?

The second part of that question was the most self-confronting to me. By the time I got to this question I knew what I wanted to be doing with my days from that point forward. But I found it so hard to let go of what I was currently working and focusing on. (I bet you can relate to that, too!)

Question #2: What is currently unfolding in your life that no longer serves you or makes you happy?

How did it go? It's tough, right? That's okay. Tough is good when the exercise is to discover your best life.

Tough means you're digging deep. Great job.

I want you to write the answers to these questions on a separate piece of paper and then tape them on the wall where you brush your teeth in the morning. Then read your answers out loud every single day because knowing your true purpose is one thing, but ingraining it into the fiber of your being through daily repetition and recognition helps you dial up to the next level of achievement. When you see those answers on the wall every the morning, you'll be driven to take action and nothing will stop you.

Beginning each day with your newfound, true purpose in mind will help you separate yourself from others in your field because you will be driven by your goals, rather than *opportunities*. Without knowing and reminding yourself of *your* true purpose, it can be easy to be get distracted by the next opportunity or veer off course for the next quick paycheck. That's why so many people are not living a life consistent with their true desires and find themselves taking turns in the wrong direction. By focusing on these daily reminders, you can stay on your path and be driven solely by your true purpose.

Before we move onto the last part of the Discover Phase in the *Right Now* framework, it's important to pause and reflect on one very important thing I haven't talked about yet, but that can help get you through some of the tougher moments as you construct your best life: Gratitude.

No matter how many falls you've taken or mistakes you've made, the fact that you're reading this means you have a lot to be grateful for, and a bright future ahead of you. Sometimes the desire for *more* or *better* or *true purpose* or *your best life* plays tricks on people's minds and convinces them their life isn't good *Right Now*.

But the opposite is true. The fact that you're reading this tells me so many great things about you. It tells me you believe a bright future is possible. It tells me you have the education and skills to consume and comprehend content like this. And it tells me you have the means to get your hands on a copy of this book. It tells me you have a lot to be grateful for, just as you are.

I take a moment each day to list several things I am grateful for and suggest you do the same. Listing all the things I have to be grateful for every day has helped me combat self-doubt, fear of failure, and unforeseen circumstances. So take a moment—*Right Now*—and write out five things in your life you're grateful for. Do it right here on this page. It doesn't matter how big or little they are, just list five things you're grateful for in your life (or things you're grateful for not having in your life, such as famine, extreme poverty, or illness). Pausing to express gratitude for little things like having clean and fresh water whenever you want, or being able to see, hear, and walk—for having the many things others lack—can give you a new perspective from which to launch into greatness!

I want you to do this on a regular basis, especially if you feel frustrated, overwhelmed, or confused. I do this many times each day because it's critical to remember that, although this book is about improving your life, you're already great and worthy, *Right Now*, just as you are. The *Right Now* process helps you harness that greatness and thrust it into a direction of your own design. Let's go.

Five things I am grateful for—*Right Now*—are
1)_____ 2)_____ 3)_____ 4)_____ 5)_____

For example, five things *I'm* grateful for *Right Now* are (1) you for reading this book and taking action to live a life of true purpose; (2) my wife, who loves and cares for me; (3) my health; (4) my espresso machine, as I sip this coffee, which tastes amazing; and (5) the ability to reach, help, and inspire others.

If you're having a hard time finding five, although this sounds crazy, try coming up with one hundred. That's what I ask my high-level consulting clients do because once you get past five or ten, you start to realize how many things we all have to be grateful for like running water, air conditioning, shoes, and shelter. Most people reading this book have those, but many people in the world do not. There's so much to be grateful for, so I highly encourage you to come back to this exercise frequently. Doing so helps you reset your mindset and get unstuck.

Take a minute to reread those five things you're grateful for. Pretty cool, right?

We have looked to the future to see how you want your life to turn out, looked to the present to identify what might not be consistent with your vision of your future, and taken time to express gratitude for what you already have. Now it's time to travel back in time to bring the Discover Phase full circle.

So let me ask you . . .

What Did You Want To Be When You Grew Up?

When I was a kid I dreamed of becoming an actor. I loved to entertain. I loved being on stage. I loved making people smile and laugh. I couldn't explain the rush it gave me at the time, but I just knew I wanted more of it. It took me a couple of decades to figure out exactly what that feeling was. That rush. It was purpose.

That rush was my brain and my heart telling me what I was doing was consistent with my mission in life. That rush was telling me entertaining, presenting, making people smile, and making people laugh was exactly what I was put on this planet to do. I just didn't know this at the time. In fact, I didn't fully come to grips with the magnitude of what that all meant until very recently.

What about you? What did you want to be when you grew up? Take a trip back to your childhood, your upbringing, your teenage years. What did you feel, desire, and maybe even seek out back then? Now look at your current situation and answer this next question.

Are you currently living the life you dreamed of when you were younger? Are you following the path you truly and deeply desired way back when?

Remember when you answer it's important not to be too literal. The real power of this exercise is that back when you were younger and you dreamed of what you'd do or what you'd become, your answers weren't limited by outside pressures or challenges. You dreamed of being something and there was a reason for it. That *reason* is what mature you, the *you* who is reading this needs to find out.

As you know by now, I wanted to be an actor, but the underlying reason for wanting to be an actor was to perform, entertain, and add value to people's lives in a way that makes them smile or laugh. And while I am not an actor in the traditional sense now, I am certainly performing, entertaining, and helping others in a meaningful way.

The vast majority of people will find that, sometime between dreaming as a child and living as an adult, they took a sharp turn and their current situation looks *nothing* like what they had dreamed of before the world pushed them around and societal pressures took over.

If you're in that majority, I have just the exercise for you. You already know what you want to be said about you at your funeral. That's your future. The answers to these questions will help you connect your past with your present and then point you in the direction of your future, as you designed it in the eulogies you drafted. This is where you start discovering some of the answers to how you'll get where you want to go.

For this exercise it's critical that you go back in time and get in "younger you's" head. Answer these questions as your younger, high school, or even college self. Doing so with 100 percent of your focus will help you get the most out of what can be a truly transformational exercise.

1. Write an age you're going back to when answering these questions? (If you're not sure, just go back to when you were ten years old.) Remember that age when answering.

2. What do you want to be when you grow up?

3. Why? What was it about that profession that makes you dream of it?

4. What problems will you solve?

5. What will your days look like?

6. Where will you be living?

7. Who do you spend the most time with?

Okay, ready to come back to the present?

Great. Welcome back. How did it go? If this is the first time you've ever gone back in time and answered questions from the standpoint of your younger self, then I am sure this was challenging and maybe a little uncomfortable.

Don't be discouraged if your childhood dream is not consistent with your current life. While this exercise does help discover the direction you can go to achieve your true self, it doesn't matter how far you've strayed because Phases 2, 3, and 4, will get you on the right track. The important part is to identify the underlying reasons for that childhood dream and use those reasons to help design a plan and develop yourself and your surroundings in a way that allows you to deliver extraordinary, meaningful results. In fact, I would go as far to say you're only one thought away from bridging the gap between your childhood dreams and a future full of great joy. You're only one thought away from that feeling, that purpose. And don't worry—I'll help you identify that one thought and then take decisive action in the right direction.

Also, while the quickest path between two points is a straight line, I challenge you to find a single person who is living the life of their dreams and faced no adversity, no misdirection, and no challenges. In other words, you're going to get bumped around a bit, and that's okay. The people who achieve true greatness are the ones who keep going, bumps and all.

Before I ever stepped on stage or helped a single person improve their lives, I had multiple jobs, multiple career paths, multiple bumps, and multiple bruises. It was only after really putting the *Right Now* framework to practice in my life that I found my final change of direction, the one that allowed me to start heading towards living the life of my dreams. You can do it, too.

Reflection

Let's take a moment to reflect on the Discover Phase before we move on to Phase 2.

1. What did you discover about yourself as you went through the exercises?

2. What was the one thing that stood out to you as being an area in your life you might want to make an immediate change in?

3. Did you discover anything you currently do on a day-to-day basis that you already know doesn't belong in your life anymore? If so, declare your commitment right here. Then put a sticky note on this page, or bend the corner over, or write in your journal, in case you need a reminder down the road.

4. Complete this sentence: Today is the __ day of _____,
_____ and I, _____, will no longer _____

_____.

For example: Today is the 17th day of April, and I, Brett
Campbell, will no longer limit myself to a mediocre life. I'll
take control of my destiny from this moment forward.

5. Did anything else stick out to you from the Discover Phase?

Now that you've worked through the Discover Phase exercises, I
strongly encourage you to journal about your findings. Put the book
down or use the blank spaces on this page and just write. Don't edit.
Just allow your mind to reflect on the exercises and write what comes to
mind, how you're feeling and what you're thinking.

You might want to get a nice, new, clean journal you dedicate to the
Right Now exercises. We will be doing many exercises throughout this
book, so it will be useful for you to keep them all in one place. If you
want some *Right Now* worksheets you can stick in a binder to make your
own *Right Now* journal you can download it for free on the resources
page (http://brettcampbell.net/right-now-resources).

Once you're done journaling about the Discover Phase come back
and get ready to design your personal process and surroundings to put
you in a position to achieve extraordinary success! Trust me, you're ready!

PHASE 2
DESIGN

CHAPTER 7

Your Personal Plan for Greatness

W hen I was nineteen I sat down at a table with a piece of paper and a pencil. I started to draw, but it didn't look right, so I scrapped it and started to draw again. The second time through was much better than the first. The third better than the second. And by the fourth, it started taking shape. After a few more trips to the trash can, I was ready. At just nineteen years old, I had just drawn a very rough floorplan for my first custom-built house.

Once I roughed out a fair representation of what I wanted, I took it to a friend who was an architect, who then turned it into an actual blueprint. What started as a few blank pieces of paper and a dream had morphed into what would soon be a home—my home.

A short while later, the day of construction had finally arrived. My design was about to become my reality. In less than two weeks, construction was finished. You read that right. From start to finish, my completed design was turned it into a livable home within two weeks.

I share this story for two reasons. First, because it demonstrates how far you can go in a quick period of time with the proper plan, hustle, and focus. Fourteen years earlier I was a five-year-old living in a motor home. After fleeing the motor home and my alcoholic, abusive father, I spent a decade in a pretty rough neighborhood, with gangs and plenty of crime. And just three years before construction began I was sitting across from my high school principal being told I needed to leave school. In three teenage years, I went from high school dropout to homeowner.

Second, I share this story because it demonstrates the power of having a plan and support. How did this come together so quickly? It wasn't magic. It was a plan and support. I had a plan from the start. It started rough, but I adjusted it and then got help finalizing it. I drew the rough sketch. My friend, the architect, cleaned it up. I also got help from a big group of friends who worked tirelessly to help me turn the sketch into a home. Right from the start, and all along the way, everyone knew exactly what was needed to build the house and to build it fast. Everyone showed up, every day. Everyone focused, every day. Everyone knew the plan, every day. And everyone followed the plan carefully, every single day.

The same is true with designing meaningful change in your life. Just like building a great house doesn't happen by accident, building and living a joyous and purposeful life doesn't happen by accident and requires living with intention, purpose, and full presence, every day.

When I was on the plane on the way back from Asri's funeral, I promised myself I would never let "life live me" and would live life to the fullest from that moment forward. I promised myself I would take control of my destiny and decide how I spent my days and who I spent them with. I committed to designing and following a life plan that was meaningful to me.

Unless you commit to designing and following a life plan that's meaningful to you, you'll be at the mercy of other people's priorities. It's your choice. You can be purposeful and go where you want to go. Or you can be passive and go wherever the wind blows you. You can be an eagle, spending your days gliding through life, observing the world below you, and deciding on your next landing spot with great focus and intention. Or, you can be a duck, spending your days waddling around everywhere, quacking away for no reason, and waiting for the next bored grandmother to come by and throw a few breadcrumbs your way.

Which would you rather be, the duck or the eagle?

The New Age of Lifestyle Design

In the Design Phase of this framework, we start to take life planning very seriously. This phase involves looking at exactly what type of life you want to live and designing the steps you can take—*Right Now*—to start heading in that direction.

We start by looking at what I call the new age of lifestyle design. This will challenge the status quo and the norms society has chosen for us for way too long. For example, who said our life needs to be designed around a nine to five working day? And when nine to five changes, who says it needs to be changed to require *more* hours and not less? Where did eight to six come from? Who said we can only have two days off each week? And who said I can only have thirty minutes for lunch?

As an entrepreneur once trapped in an employee's mindset, I have been there and experienced those frustrations. I worked a seven-to-five job, five to six days a week, in a dusty, cold factory doing something I knew I didn't want to be doing for the rest of my life. I did it for five years. For five long years I allowed this to be my reality. I justified it by telling myself I was a twenty-two-year-old high school dropout with a mortgage and no idea what I really wanted to do with my life. I had no idea what I wanted to do and had a big financial commitment I had made a few years earlier. So I stuck around at a job I didn't like, working hours I didn't want to work, and seemingly living the same tired day over and over again, month after month, year after year. Looking back, it was way too easy to justify trading years of my life because of a financial commitment and lack of direction.

At the time it just felt easier to put up with the pain than to face it and do something different. I performed well and was being groomed to take over as an owner of the business one day, or so I thought. So there was some vague sense of progress, even if it was buried deep below a big pile of misery. I figured, if I didn't know what I wanted to do next, I might as well stay somewhere familiar and where I had some possibility for progressing up the corporate ladder. I wasn't in any real danger of losing my job, so I also had some sense of stability, even if the stability was stable lack of enthusiasm. It wasn't until the pain of going to work every day reached a point where I could no longer handle even thinking about going to work anymore that I finally mustered up the courage to take a leap and embark on my next journey.

I wasn't entirely sure what I wanted to do, right away, but I did know I had an interest in becoming a professional fitness trainer. At that point I had recently turned twenty-three, still had that mortgage, and was no longer earning any money. I needed to make this next move count. So I decided to take out a pile of student loans and enroll in some classes at the local university to help me become a professional fitness trainer.

I quickly realized going deeply into debt to attend college was not the best decision. Although I did confirm my interest in the fitness industry, the process of going through a full university education was just not a good fit. I was made to study subjects that I had no interest in, with no connection to my goals, just to check some boxes in the university's curriculum. On top of that, the materials in the subjects I was actually interested in were so slowly drip-fed that I felt I was going in reverse. The only thing that was adding up fast was the debt. I wasn't going to make the same mistake twice like I did with my last job by sticking around way too long.

I knew I needed to pivot quickly, so at the end of the first year, I dropped out, hopped on a plane with a suitcase in one hand and my golf clubs in the other, and moved from New Zealand to Australia to start a new life. I was committed to not wasting time somewhere that wasn't a good fit for me, even with a pile of student debt.

That year at the university wasn't a total waste of time, though. Although I didn't get much out of the classes, I learned quite a bit about lifestyle and efficiency that still serves me well today. It was also a great break from the fifty-hour work week I had worked for the five years before that. I liked that, for that year, I went to one to two classes a day, then spent the rest of the day either at the gym or hanging out with friends. It was the exact opposite experience from everything I had known since I dropped out of high school.

The next big decision I had to make was what I was going to do in Australia. I started thinking about what I was good at, which in high school was three things: woodwork, physical education, and lunch. I had spent half a decade doing woodwork and knew that wasn't the right fit for me. And there were not too many options for getting paid to eat, so I thought the only thing left was to continue to pursue becoming a fitness professional, just not in a university setting.

It wasn't much of a plan, but at least it was a direction relating to something I enjoyed and was really good at, right?

After a little investigation I discovered a correspondence course I could complete in a matter of months, instead of four years, because it focused on fitness education, rather than requiring unrelated core courses. That's right, I could become a qualified fitness professional without thousands of additional dollars in student loans. I learned everything I needed to know about the fitness world, but I didn't need to take—or pay for—calculus! After a few of those *I wish I had known about this sooner* moments, I dove in. I could see a plan taking shape. I studied during the day and worked at a local nightclub at night. In a matter of months, I completed my qualifications, landed a job in a big gym, and learned an extremely valuable lesson.

Just a short time earlier, I planned to be at a full-time university for four years, piling up thousands and thousands of dollars in student loans, with the hope of becoming a fitness professional while at the same time, a much faster and cost-effective alternative was sitting there waiting for me. It took a pretty gutsy decision to leave the university early without much of a plan and with a bunch of student loans. But in taking that action and then looking for other ways to achieve the same goal, I found a better way.

In fact, I was already earning a full-time income doing exactly the job I went to the university to qualify for before any of my friends from the university had started their second year of studies. They were still spending money while I was earning money doing what I wanted to do.

Once I had my new job, I started working very slowly on designing the rest of my life. I liked that at the university I could work out and hang out with my friends while I studied, and I wanted that same level of fulfillment with my new career, so I set a goal to never have to work a Friday again. I wasn't sure exactly how I would pull it off, but this was a big deal to me and would be a massive achievement to pull it off.

Having just discovered a way to trade four years of university for an eight-week certification, I felt a bit empowered. So I started planning, and implementing, and came up with a plan.

The lesson here is you may be in a situation, *Right Now*, in which you feel like you have to finish something you started because you don't know of another way to achieve the same result. If you start looking for other options, you may be surprised to find other, better ways to accomplish what you're looking to do. Don't wait for it to rain. Go find the rain, jump in the puddles, and make waves.

The *Right Now* Calendar Method of Lifestyle Design

The first step to designing your life is to get a piece of paper, a pen or pencil, a current-year calendar, and several markers of different colors. I recommend at least five colors. Although it's not mandatory to have different colors, if you're visual like me it will help you a lot. If you don't have a calendar handy you can download one for free on the resources page at http://brettcampbell.net/right-now-resources.

As you get ready for the exercise it's important for you to get into the right mindset. Enter this exercise as an optimist. From this point forward the glass is either half-full or overflowing! You see only the opportunities and are blind to the challenges. You're to dedicate 100 percent of your positive energy to this exercise. We are about to design your ideal year! Don't hold back.

The first thing I want you to do is to take your piece of paper and make a list of all the important things you want to do or achieve in the next year. If you're starting this in the middle of the year, that's okay, just work with the time you have left for this current year or print out twelve monthly calendars from the resources page and design the next twelve months.

Vacation Time

The next thing I want you to plan is vacation time. Start where you want to be. I want you to plan more vacations than you could ever imagine taking in the next year. Your vacations will be the first thing you mark on the calendar. This is imperative. Who doesn't want a vacation anyway, right?

Vacations are critical for revitalizing our minds and bodies and making the best use of our time. Yet when I run this exercise with my high-performance coaching clients for the first time, you'd think I was asking them to schedule a weekly exploratory colonoscopy. Most of them have never looked at their year like this before, especially when I direct them to schedule at least five full weeks off. I urge them to take more than that, of course, but we start with five weeks.

At this point they, and probably you too, are either very excited about the idea of first scheduling at least five full weeks of vacation or are frozen by self-doubt and fear.

I have heard all of the excuses, although they usually fall into two categories:

- "Five weeks? But I don't own my own business yet, Brett. I only get three weeks of vacation time a year," or
- "Five weeks? I can't afford five weeks of vacation Brett. You're crazy!"

You're right. You'll never be given five weeks off from your job and you'll never be able to afford five weeks of vacation—if you allow that thought process to become your reality. What's key here is to do your best with what you have. Plan more vacation than you're comfortable with.

I get it. For some people five weeks, even ten weeks, is no problem. For others, even one day off can be a mission. Most of the time, though, if you peel back the onion, the real reasons people don't take vacation has nothing to do with money. Most of the time, the real reason is disorganization and lack of commitment to making it happen. Other times, they think taking a vacation needs to be taking a plane around the world to a five-star all-inclusive resort. You can get to that point, but here we are just talking about taking time off. I don't care what you do. I only care that you plan to do it and then do it. For all I care, you can swap houses with a friend from a few towns over for a week, as long as you're out of your routine and rejuvenating your heart and mind. Even a "staycation" will suffice.

Don't worry about the details yet. By the end of this process you'll be motivated and equipped to get creative. For example, when I was working full-time as a cabinetmaker, I wanted to take a five-week trip around Europe with my best friend, but my job gave me only three weeks of vacation time each year.

I had a plan to sit down with my boss, face-to-face, and convince him to let me take five weeks off instead of three for this special trip. I was not going to let the small issue of some technical three-week rule get in between me and the experience of a lifetime. The day came and I was ready, or at least I thought I was. Early in the day I asked my boss for ten minutes with him to discuss something important. He agreed. When the time came I walked into his office and said I wanted to take five weeks off for a once-in-a-lifetime trip and had an idea as to how to manage it from a business perspective.

His immediate response was to push back. "You only have three weeks of vacation time and we can't really afford to have you away that long," was his initial reaction. By that point I had become the factory foreman in charge of six guys and we were right in the middle of a massive growth phase.

Hearing that, the vast majority of people would allow their dream to be derailed, walking out of the office with their head down and accepting they tried, but it just wasn't in the cards. But not me. I already knew I only had three weeks. I knew I was busy all day, every day and being gone would be a challenge for the business. I knew all of that before I proposed a five-week vacation and went into the room intent on doing whatever I had to do to make it happen.

But he offered me a lifeline. "So what's your plan?" he asked. "I realize I only have three weeks of paid leave per year, which leaves me two weeks short, or about ninety to one hundred hours short. I have five months before I want to take this trip, or about twenty weeks, so I propose to work Saturdays and any other hours that become available, at least an extra five per week or one hundred total, before I leave, with no extra pay. You pay me for those days with regular pay during the two extra vacation weeks."

Right as I was about to finish a voice interrupted us. "Brett! You already used one week this year, so you'll be three weeks short, not two!" shouted the office administrator from the other room.

GULP! The conversation was not heading in a good direction. My first reaction was to suggest that we just change the math. Instead of five extra hours per week I would have to work seven or eight. I was certainly willing to do that. But my boss was not willing to budge.

At that point I had a decision to make. I had built up a lot of good will over the years and I knew I only had a few options left at that point. First, I could just accept it and leave. Second, I could look for another job that either gave me more leave or where I could negotiate having the time off for the trip during the interview process. Or, I could take all of the good will I had built up over the years and go all in. Perhaps because I was still relatively young and did not have any mouths to feed but my own (although I did have a mortgage), I decided to go all in.

"I understand this is an unusual request," I said, "but this is also an unusual opportunity. I need to take this trip and if you can't approve the time off, even with me working the extra hours before I leave, I do understand, but I'll have to leave."

Silence. I had just moved all of my chips into the middle of the table and my boss held all the cards except for one: my years of service. If he couldn't envision three additional weeks without me, maybe he would consider those three weeks as a lesser of two evils and make a one-time exception.

The problem was I didn't want to leave either. Although I didn't like the job very much and my discomfort was rising on a daily basis, I did have a mortgage and did not have another source of income at the time.

I just wanted to take a vacation of a lifetime. I didn't want it to turn into a job hunt.

When the silence broke my boss agreed to think about it. It wasn't a "no." That was good enough for me.

That afternoon my boss approved my request.

I share this story with you not to suggest you should walk into your boss's office and demand more vacation or you'll leave (although if you can do that respectfully and without ditching responsibilities like putting food on the table for your family it would be pretty amazing). I share it as an example of someone doing whatever they needed to do to make the impossible possible. I share it to push you a little bit out of your comfort zone, to encourage you to honor your responsibilities, but to start doing things differently.

Maybe getting out of *your* comfort zone involves just taking the vacation time you're entitled to for once. Maybe getting out of your comfort zone means asking to work remotely one day a week (or month).

So, take this challenge with me, schedule the vacation time, and address the details later. Pay attention to your emotions while you're doing it. Allow yourself the time to dream, to construct your year without worrying about the challenges you currently have in your life. You have time to figure out the details, to think differently, and to get creative. The rest of the book will help, too. For the purposes of this exercise, you may want to think of "you" as a third person. Design that person's year as if they had all the hopes, dreams, and experiences as you, but none of the constraints. Deal?

After scheduling your vacations for the next twelve months, here are the next three things to mark on the calendar.

Long Weekends

This is pretty straightforward but so often overlooked. Don't wait for a "public holiday" that's chosen by some governmental body to give you permission to have a long weekend. And if you work for yourself, don't fall into the trap of working 24/7/365. I have been there. It's crazy. It literally feels like there's no off switch. But scheduling long weekends gives you a nice quick jolt of energy and rejuvenation. And that's why this is so important. In fact, you'll likely find you get more done in those four-day weeks than you do in the typical five-day week. So schedule at least five long weekends. And mix them up. Sometimes take a Friday. Other times, a Monday. See what works for you. If you're an overachiever, I dare you to schedule one long weekend a month. And if you already schedule long weekends, add a few. Take it to the next level. Maybe try a few four-day weekends.

Be creative if you have to. If you work for someone else, maybe you can try starting to work at home on a Friday afternoon. Or, if your job can't be done at home, maybe you can ask to leave work at lunchtime on a Friday and catch a movie, play a round of golf, or have an afternoon date with your spouse. Maybe you can work four ten-hour days instead of five eight-hour days. You get the point.

If you make it happen I guarantee your life will never be the same again. You'll see work differently. You'll see time differently.

A word of caution with this one. Don't let what you think your boss will say stand in your way. Both with weekends and with the vacation time, a lot of folks get so stuck with what they think their boss will say they give up right away. For example, a friend of mine was adamant that his boss would never let him have Friday afternoons off because they were always busy and they needed him to be there as much as possible. I pushed back, asking whether his boss had actually said that or if he just presumed he would say that. "No, he didn't say it," he answered. "I just know that's what he would say."

Like I usually do, I suggested he take some time to get in his boss's shoes for a minute and devise an approach that his boss might connect with. "Then, just ask him," I suggested. "What's the worst that can happen? He proves you right by saying no? Are you concerned about how you might look if you ask him?" That last one hit the mark. He thought his boss would think he is lazy or not committed to his job. It's the big struggle with being in an employment situation. On the one hand, you don't want to dedicate your life to your job. But on the other, you don't want to get fired, so you become so concerned about what your boss or coworkers *might* think you forget or give up on pursuing what is most important to *you*.

But he agreed to ask. And guess whose boss gave him the next four Fridays off completely, with pay, with the only caveat that he hit his targets and get his work done Monday through Thursday? You guessed it. You can do it, too.

It's all in the mindset and the approach.

Rejuvenation Days

The next thing I want you to calendar is four rejuvenation days, ideally once a quarter. If you're not familiar with the concept, rejuvenation days are days where you simply turn everything off, allow your internal systems to cool down and get some much needed rest. No technology is allowed. All power buttons are off. And you let no disturbances in, just calmness and peace.

It took me a while to realize the true importance of rejuvenation days. From the day I was born I was "foot to the floor." I had one gear and it was full-speed ahead. It's the same for most entrepreneurs, high achievers, and especially mothers. But the more you think you can't take a rejuvenation day, the more you actually need one. Mothers need this day more than most people. They spend 99 percent of their days catering to other people's needs and are one bad moment from breaking down. They need this rejuvenation. They need time to focus on themselves. If you're a mother, I really hope you take this concept to heart. If not,

I hope you can help create an environment to support the mothers in your world. Help one have her rejuvenation day. Volunteer to take her kids for a day and take care of all the details ahead of time so she can enjoy a full day of rejuvenation.

If you're a single parent, get a babysitter, relative, or friend to help you out. Swap kids with another mother for a day, so each of you can rejuvenate. As you know by now, making these days happen is all about your mindset. So for now, simply mark at least one day down every three months as your rejuvenation day.

Relationship Days

Like rejuvenation days, relationship days are meant to help you connect better with loved ones. The obvious example is your spouse, of course, but it doesn't have to be limited to just your spouse. Yes, please schedule relationships days with your spouse if you have one. But if not, schedule some days to spend quality time with other significant people in your life, like kids, parents, friends, or cousins.

I schedule at least fifty-two relationship days with my wife each year. Every Wednesday is our relationship day. It's not always something elaborate and can be anything from dinner and a movie to a home spa day, with a spa bath, some candles, music, and some dedicated time to focus on each other. We focus on both being present every relationship date. We treat it with the intention and thoughtfulness as if it were our first date. I try to be cute, charming, and funny, and she smiles and laughs at all my bad jokes. Alright, maybe she actually finds them funny. Either way, we have a lot of fun.

I want you to schedule at least twenty-six relationship days, one every other week. *Right Now.*

While this might sound like the all-too-common, and often skipped, "date night" so many people talk about, it's way more. Relationship days are scheduled intentionally. They are etched in stone. They are not skipped. And the intention and presence you give to relationship days is above and beyond any mechanical "date night."

Now that you've scheduled twenty-six relationship days on your calendar I want you to circle at least six of them, at least every two months for a full-day next-level relationship day. These are full-day, super focused, smile-inducing, memory-creating days you dedicate to sharing experiences with the loved one of choice. My wife and I book a hotel somewhere and simply get away for a long weekend (See what I did there? The days are crossing over!). If you choose not to invest in a hotel or you don't have the money for one, buy or borrow a tent and go camping (we have done that as well). Or get silly at home. Heck, I have even built a fortress with blankets and pillows right in our living room and asked my wife to hang out with me right there. Yes, a grown man built a fortresses of blankets and pillows in his living room. And, yes, his wife actually got in! It also didn't hurt that I lured her in with chocolate . . . .

The key here is to adopt the mindset of doing whatever you need to do to make this happen. The time and the focus are the two most valuable parts of relationship days. The details are just details.

So circle at least six of those twenty-six relationship days. Now step back for a minute.

Here are two more days I highly recommend adding. I could go on for some time with rewarding days to schedule, but the point is not necessarily *what* you schedule. The point is to schedule, to spend your time intentionally. The items we talk about here will provide a good start for you to build momentum and take control.

1. Education Days: Attend live events with like-minded people. I'd be honored to meet you, so check out my speaking schedule so we can connect. Look for other opportunities close to home and far away. You may find single or multiday conferences in an

area that would make a great vacation spot. Having several days of vacation after a great conference is an incredible way to start implementing the lessons right away.

2. Give-Back Days: Volunteer at a charity, school, sports team, or other event that's important to you. These types of organizations are always looking for help.

What Now?

Now that you've marked your calendar with these important days, it's time to add your personal days. (Notice we are still not focused on anyone but you and your loved ones.) Add all of the birthdays, anniversaries, milestones, events, etc., that are important to you and your family.

Congratulations! You just completed your personal growth calendar! Now leave it alone. Don't second-guess the days you put in there. There will be time for tweaks. But, for now, just know you at least momentarily are putting your personal priorities first and that's awesome.

When all is said and done and you're looking back at your life, I don't want you to have any regrets, starting *Right Now.* I realize there are probably some things that have happened in your past that you wouldn't do again, but you had a different mindset then. Don't worry. Move forward with a fresh start. Now that you have a new mindset you're ready to take personal responsibility to make positive, meaningful changes that can not only transform your life, but also transform the lives of your loved ones.

Now that we've taken care of you, let's work on your surroundings.

CHAPTER 8

Are Your Surroundings Sabotaging Your Success?

When I think back to my high school teacher putting my desk in the hallway, I know her intent was to both punish me and also remove me as a distraction to others. Looking back, however, there was also a major advantage to me. I didn't know it at the time, but in many ways, my desk in the hallway was a small version of the Design Phase of the *Right Now* framework. I just hadn't planned it myself. How?

When my desk was in the room, I was not only a distraction to others, but I was also distracted myself. My surroundings were not ideal for me to learn in a way that worked for me. Once I got in the hallway though, I'd get my work done within the first ten minutes, as opposed to never completing it or taking a very long time. During the other forty-five minutes I would draw pictures, make paper airplanes, or be designing my next tree hut, but for those first ten minutes, I was in the zone. I felt great, at least for those ten minutes, the other forty-five minutes felt more like a prison sentence. And as you can see, I didn't make great use of that time at all, although I can make a pretty awesome paper airplane now.

But what if I could take the lessons learned from having my desk in the hallway and apply them to my limitless dreams, which wouldn't cause me to run out of things to do after ten minutes? The answer is not only that I could do a lot more. The answer is I could achieve more meaning for myself and others.

When I first shared this concept with one of my coaching clients, who struggled to get work done at home, I was shocked both at the environment in which he was trying to work as well as the impact this shift in mindset could have on what was a challenging situation. He was looking for productivity hacks, an all-too-common term these days, but I knew he needed more than a few productivity tips.

"What is the environment like where you're trying to get work done?" I asked. At first, he must have been questioning whether I had actually been paying attention to anything he'd been telling me from the time we started working together. "What do you mean?" he asked. "I work from home. You know that." "Yes, I *do*," I assured him, "but what is your home environment like?"

"Well, I have an office that's separate from the rest of the house. Although my kids do run around all day, they only interrupt me a few times each day," he answered. "Anything else? Any other disruptions?" I asked. "Yeah, my wife likes to come in and chat a bit." I was convinced that no *hack* would help. He needed a full surroundings makeover. It was time for me to push him a little bit more.

Your surroundings can either make or break your success. Success, for this conversation with my coaching client, was to get more done. For you, it might be to get to the gym more or to see your sister more often, or to eat healthier, or finish school. Without the right surroundings you're starting with a severe disadvantage.

So think hard about your surroundings and how they contribute to or take away from your ability to achieve your true purpose. Do it *Right Now*. Picture yourself walking into this area, and then answer these questions:

- What thoughts come into your mind when you're in there?
- Are you worried about anything?
- How do you feel?
- Are you confident?
- How much energy do you have?
- How excited are you to enter this space, on a scale of one to ten?
- What would you add to the space to improve it if you could add anything at all?
- What else?
- What would you remove from the space if you could remove anything?
- What else?

When I went through this exercise with my client, he was shocked. He felt overwhelmed when he was in his office. He was demotivated by it. And he actually said he *hated* going in there. *Hated?* What about excitement? "Probably about a three or four out of ten," he admitted.

It was settled. He didn't need hacks, he needed to set up his environment for success, not failure. Every day when he walked into the office he was essentially working with one eye closed and one hand tied behind his back.

We got to work, right away, designing an environment where he felt empowered and excited when he walked in, a place that made him feel smarter every time he worked there. It was pretty amazing. Just the thought of working in such an environment got him more motivated than he had been in a long time.

Designing the Perfect Working Environment

I had a very similar story with my first business, which I started in a small bedroom in a house I was renting with two friends. My desk was an old, tattered, beat-up wooden desk I found on the side of the road, destined for the trash. For a year, my office was in that tiny bedroom. I had no other option, or so I thought. I finally got into a situation where I moved into another rental with an extra bedroom that could function as an office. It was such an amazing feeling to make that transition. I noticed an immediate uptick in productivity and my mindset with just that one change in surroundings.

As the company grew and we started building a team, however, we wanted to expand beyond a bedroom in a house. After a brief search we found a two-story building with okay office space on the top floor and plenty of storage on the bottom floor, so we signed a lease and moved in. The new office was much bigger than the old one in the bedroom. I was *so* ready to take my productivity to the next level.

I thought having a real office and a lot more space I would be able to accomplish way more than before. Unfortunately, this didn't turn out to be the case. In fact, it was just the opposite.

Yes, my office was bigger, but it was also colder and darker. I didn't really want to be there. There I was, just a few weeks into a two-year lease, and I wanted nothing to do with my office space. I was unproductive and unmotivated. I needed to take action.

I think you know me well enough by now to know what I did next. I grabbed a pencil and paper and started over from scratch to lay out my ideal environment. Just like I did with my first house, I designed my perfect environment, right down to the very words and pictures I would hang on the walls. I didn't limit myself in my thinking. I wanted an area where I would feel comfortable. I wanted a room that would give me a hug every time I walked in it. (Weird, I know.)

My ideal working space had a big bookshelf, three desks, and whiteboards on the walls. It had a nice big window with a beautiful view that captured the morning sun. It had a whisper-quiet air conditioner for the hot months and a similarly silent heater for the cold ones. And to top it off, it needed to be very close to home. Ideally, it would be *in* my home.

Just completing that exercise lifted a lot of the weight off my shoulders because I now had a plan, a target. (This is one of the major benefits of the Design Phase of the *Right Now* framework. It's empowering.)

So now I had the perfectly designed office but I was stuck. I had four employees and a two-year office lease. I didn't want to break the lease, which would cost thousands of dollars.

But then something unusual (okay, disastrous) happened. Just a few weeks after we moved into our new office space, the landlord of the house I was living in called and said we had to move out in a month!

I was so stressed I actually contemplated moving into the ugly office space to live! It was then I decided it was time to buy a home again—I had wasted enough money on rent and being at the mercy of a landlord.

To make matters worse, it was only a few weeks until Christmas—not the best time of year to be house shopping—especially on such a tight schedule.

I called up a realtor and booked a house viewing the very next day. It wasn't a good match, but the neighborhood was great, so I asked the realtor if she had any more properties in the area. She had one. And although it wasn't going to be listed for five days, she agreed to show it to us the next morning.

The house looked promising, seeming to tick all the boxes on our wish list, as we walked through the house. And then I saw it.

It was the *exact* room I had designed just a few days earlier. It hugged me as I walked in. It was warm and cozy. It had room for three desks, a big bookshelf, and white-boards. It had a big window with sun shining through. Right outside the window was a beautiful view of a large palm tree and other exotic plants. There was only one more thing to look for, the air conditioner.

I checked all the windows. No air conditioner. I checked all the walls. No air conditioner. And then I saw it. Right there in the ceiling, a bright white vent. It had central air conditioning. I was sold.

I know it sounds a bit crazy, but we decided to break the office lease, I would move my office into the (perfect) office in the house, and our employees would work virtually.

But the great news was it turned out we didn't have to pay any money to break the lease because the landlord found new tenants right away! It was a true win/win/win. We had new a new home/office; our home landlord had new tenants; and the office had new tenants.

Our productivity went up and surprisingly, our employee's productivity went up as well.

Now I'm not suggesting you go out and buy a big new home (unless you want to!) or that by simply drawing a picture of your ideal environment the universe will magically deliver it to you. But I do know in order to excel and live a joyful and meaningful life, you need an environment that contributes to you and your mission.

It's quite simple. Your environment affects your mood. Your mood affects your output. And your output affects your results. By creating an environment you can't wait to get to, or at the very least love being in, you're automatically putting yourself in a position to succeed from the start.

Now that you understand the importance of a supportive environment, free of negative emotions, constant interruptions, noisy air conditioners, or whatever else takes away from your productivity and motivation, I'll help you design the three major surroundings you must pay attention to in order to be in a position to succeed. In the next chapter, you will apply the principles learned in this chapter, along with the knowledge you discovered about yourself in Phase 1, to your surroundings, and by doing that you'll be putting yourself in a position for some major positive changes in your life.

I'm sure it might be some type of record to go from deciding to buy a house and then making a purchase only two days later. That was some feat, even for me. But I was motivated and had a tight deadline. I learned from that experience that when a deadline approaches, all the "ums" and "ahhhs" and self-doubt many people let creep into their minds and steal their time and energy disappear. Decisions become based on cold, hard facts and not emotions. I had my vision and list of must-haves. I found a house that checked the boxes and was in my budget, and I bought it. It was that simple.

When in your life have you put off making a decision you could easily have made if you had a deadline looming? Next time you come across a decision like that, I highly encourage you to make a decision and move on. I've been doing that for some time now, giving myself a deadline to make a decision, gathering information in that time, making a decision, and moving on. It helps me keep the time and energy that goes into decision making much, much smaller. Give yourself a deadline. By doing this, you'll reduce decision fatigue and get rid of a lot of stress and clutter in your brain.

CHAPTER 9

Designing Your Surroundings

World-renowned motivational and peak performance coach, Tony Robbins, says if you "change your state . . . you will change your life." I wholeheartedly agree. But I also believe if you change your *environment* you will change your life. In this chapter, I identify three key environments you must pay attention to if you want to live a full life.

Home Environment – The Humble Oasis

I was talking with a guy at a conference about how I was in the middle of a six-week trip across the United States. "Wow," he said. "You must love this. I'd love to get away from home for that long."

"You must really hate home then?" I replied. "I do like to travel, but not as much as I love the environment I have created at home."

He had never looked at it that way. Not many people do. For many people, home is where you'll spend most of your time. That's exactly why it's so important you make it the most beneficial, meaningful, and joyful place possible.

So even if you've never thought of your home as anything more than a stack of sticks to keep the rain off of your head, I can help you design the perfect home environment. The first step is to answer these three questions on a scale of one to ten.

- How happy do you feel when you think about your home environment? ___ /10
- When you're in this environment, are you being your true and best self? ___ /10
- How much time and effort have you put into creating an amazing home environment? ___ /10

If you scored at least a twenty-seven out of thirty then I would like an invitation to your home! It would be awesome to hang out with you there. Now ask yourself what you'd need to include or remove to advance to a perfect thirty? Anything less than twenty-seven and it's time to get serious designing your perfect home environment. This is way too important to settle for less.

To do so you'll need to answer these additional questions, which will walk you through your senses as you walk through your home. This will help you identify areas to enhance and things to remove. You'll get the most out of this exercise if you do it room by room to optimize each space for what it is because no two rooms have the same feel and purpose, right? Ready? Answer the following to become one step closer to creating your humble oasis:

See: What items would I love to see in my home environment and why? (In the coming pages we will look at the impact of color and its effects on your environment.)

Smell: What smells would I like to smell and why?

Hear: What sounds would I like to hear and why?

Touch: What type of furniture, flooring, water pressure, textures, and temperature do I desire?

Feel: How do I want to feel when I walk into each room of my humble oasis? (If after creating your surroundings you do not get the feelings you desire, keep going until you do.)

Spend some quiet time answering these questions in detail. Start with one room of your house and work your way through.

In each room ask yourself what you can add and remove to transform the space. Give yourself full creative license. Dream big at first to create a home you'll never want to leave. If you want a water feature in your front entrance, write it down. If you want a nice big fluffy rug under your feet in your living room, write it down. Don't worry about making it happen yet. We are talking about your ideal environment. We are in the Design Phase. Delivery is not relevant yet, although a great way to start slowly is to get rid of things you no longer want. Sell them for money to buy the additions; trade them for additions that fit your design; do whatever it takes to start moving towards your ideal home environment. At this point you have your design to work towards. You can start introducing even one item at a time, perhaps focusing on one room at a time. You'll get there.

I first taught this concept at a live event. Two days later, I received an email from one of the participants who, in just two days, rearranged or restyled his lounge, bathroom, dining room, and bedroom. He added lamps, candles, and plants, and decluttered. "Feels empowering," he said. Now that's what I call taking action!

Working Environment

Whether you work from home or at an office, work for yourself or someone else, or are a student or stay-at-home parent, you have a working environment. I am convinced the reason most people dread going to work is because they know they are leaving a piece of themselves at home. The key, therefore, to a positive work experience is to design an environment that works well for each employee. Gone are the days where you get peak efficiency by stuffing as many people as you can into a sea of monotone cubicles. In its place is a working environment that fits each employee's unique needs.

But don't take it from me, take it from Tony Hsieh, CEO of Zappos, which sold recently to Amazon for over $1.2 billion. In his book, *Delivering Happiness*, Hsieh explained that Zappos employees are given full creative license to build a working environment that pleases them. They also created themed interview rooms where candidates are more likely to relax and respond more effectively to questions, show their personality, and express their creativity. He adds, "You should let your employees take risks and try new things. Some will work and some won't and that's OK. Let your employees bring all of themselves to their job."

In order to function at your peak level as you work towards living your best life, you must design a working environment that supports your efforts. To begin, take a moment to answer the following questions related to your working environment on a scale of one to ten.

- How happy do you feel when you think about your working environment? ____ /10
- When you're in this environment, are you bringing your best and true self? ____ /10
- How much time and effort have you put into creating an amazing working environment? ____ /10

If you scored at least a twenty-seven then you're doing extremely well. Now ask yourself what you'd need to include or remove to advance to a perfect thirty? If you scored less than twenty-seven, start *Right Now* to design an improved working environment.

Start by asking yourself these questions:

- What can I add to allow for maximum productivity and happiness?
- What can I remove to improve productivity and happiness?

Give yourself full creative license to construct the perfect working environment. Make sure the environment excites, motivates, and inspires you to show up and do your best work. Your working environment is where you spend the bulk of the time you plan and execute your life's mission. It's where you create and sell the products and services that improve other people's lives, too.

My working environment helps me change the lives of hundreds of thousands of people all over the world. I take it very seriously because the more motivated, excited, and efficient I am when I am working, the more people's lives I can help change for the better.

If you work for someone else and you've already dismissed this concept of creating your perfect working environment, I encourage you to not give up. Go to your boss and explain what you want to do. Be sure you explain why and how this will benefit them with increased productivity. Be creative in your approach. Maybe start small. Or just give your boss this book to read, because they clearly need it more than you do!

As with your home environment, I am not suggesting a total overhaul of your working environment (unless you think you need it). Start small. Start simple. But start, *Right Now*.

To help you, here are a few suggestions for ways to improve your working environment:

1. New photos of your loved ones (This acts as a reminder of the reasons you're working so hard.)

2. Motivational imagery (Words are extremely powerful and have a tremendous ability to drive people to action, especially when they are connected to a personal message.)

3. A new office chair (Physical comfort is important for longevity.)

4. Plants (Plants bring a great level of ambiance to any room.)

5. A standing desk (This can reduce back pain and stress from sitting all day.)

6. Scented candles (These can evoke positive feelings. Just be sure to discuss these with your colleagues first.)

7. Better filing system (This can reduce clutter and messes on your desk and in your mind.)

8. Adjust the temperature (Do you like it hotter or colder than it is now?)

9. Lighting (Maybe the room needs to be lighter or darker.)

10. Noise reduction or addition (Ambient music in the background can help with focus and enjoyment.)

11. Color (Frank Mahnke, author of *Color, Environment, & Human Response* says, when done correctly, workers will be able to get a different visual depending on which way they are facing during the course of the day.) As you decorate your office, keep these color associations in mind:

    Yellow: stimulating, bright, cozy

    Red: arousing, fiery, aggressive

    White: open, neutral, sterile

    Green: calming and soothing

    Grey: intellect and wisdom, which might be just the look you're going for in your office.

    Blue: peaceful and tranquil. One of the most popular colors, blue causes the body to produce calming chemicals, the opposite of the body's reaction to red. Blue is often used in bedrooms (be aware that blue can also be cold and depressing), and people are often more productive in blue rooms.

In interior design, color is seen as the easiest change to make to the character of the environment. Color is also useful in subconsciously influencing human behavior, decision making, health, and much more. It provides a subtle stimulation with salient impact and has been affecting human lives physically, psychologically, physiologically, and sociologically for years.

By understanding the psychology behind creating an effective environment using all five senses, you'll begin to see a measurable and noticeable difference in the quality of life in your working environment.

But what about your creative environment?

Creative Environment

Working in the right creative environment can make a big difference. When I'm creating, dreaming, mapping things out, one of my favorite places to go is to my local coffee shop, which is full of great people and energy. I am writing these words from another place where my creativity flows well. I type these words while sitting in my reclining chair, legs fully extended, soothing music in the background, the lights slightly dimmed to take the edge off, and my green tea within arm's reach. This is one of the many creative environments I have in my home. Yes, I have many.

The specific creative environment I go to often depends on the type of project or my mood when I want to brainstorm or just do some creative thinking. If I want to take up a lot of physical space and draw things out, the large whiteboard in my office is one of my favorite spots. When I don't need a large physical space and just want to think creatively, I take my motorcycle on a cruise to one of my favorite nature locations or stay home and sit silently in my reclining chair. I sit on benches overlooking the ocean and at times even rent space or a hotel room if I need a unique setting to help me get the type of creativity and motivation I am looking for.

That may sound a little over the top, but I can assure you the ideas for our best products and services have all come from being in one of my many creative areas. You need creative space for your brain to function at its fullest.

To start identifying or improving an environment to help you take your creativity to the next level, start by asking yourself these questions and answering on a scale of one to ten. (If you do not have an established creative space just yet, give yourself a zero. That's okay, a zero means you have a blank slate!)

- How happy do you feel when you're in your creative environment? ___ /10
- When you're in your creative environment, are you being your true and best self? ___ /10
- How much time and effort have you put into creating an amazing creative environment? ___ /10

If you scored less than a twenty-seven on these questions, it's time to start designing your new and improved creative environments. Start by listing your current creative environments and a few more you believe would make you feel happy, true to yourself, and free to create. If you do not have any, just list a few places where you can start creating.

Congratulations! You've now identified spaces that only the most successful people in the world take time to cultivate.

Reflection

Now let's reflect on the Design Phase of the *Right Now* framework:

- What did you discover about yourself as you went through the exercises?
- What was the one thing that stood out to you as something you can do to make an immediate positive impact on your life?
- Anything else stick out to you from the Design Phase?

Now that you've gone through the Design Phase exercises, I strongly encourage you to journal about what you have learned about yourself, your schedule, and your surroundings. Don't edit. Just allow your mind to reflect on the exercises and write what comes to mind. If you used a different place than on these pages, use the same notepad you used for the Discover Phase so you can start to see it all come together.

Congratulations! You've come further than nine out of ten people ever will in their entire lives. You've discovered your true purpose in life in Phase 1, the Discover Phase. You've designed your personal lifestyle with more scheduled vacations, long weekends, rejuvenation days, and relationship days, and identified how to create or improve the three key surroundings for success in Phase 2, the Design Phase.

Now it's time to develop the personal traits and support network to achieve true greatness in Phase 3, the Develop Phase.

PHASE 3
DEVELOP

CHAPTER 10

Develop Your Best "Self"

The Develop Phase addresses two areas of your life you must develop to start living the abundant and fulfilled life you've just finished designing: Yourself and Your Support. The importance of having a strong understanding of and control over yourself, along with the support of key people around you can't be overstated. In this phase we take a deep dive into each of these areas of your life to give you the clarity and confidence you need to put your plan into action.

Developing your best "self" requires acknowledging, addressing, and creating action plans for each of the four areas, which I call the Four Ps. The Four Ps are the personal traits that will make or break your plan to improve your life. Have well-developed Ps and you're well on your way to maximum impact. Struggle in one or more areas and you'll struggle to improve your life as well. First, I'll introduce each of the Four Ps. Then I'll walk you through how to improve each one of them.

The Four Ps:

Psychology: The study of your mind and behavior

Physiology: The integrated behavior of your entire body

Personal Knowledge: Your ability to learn, know, and grow

Productivity: The measure of the efficiency with which you produce

Because each of the Four Ps has the power to make or break you, I'll spend a little more time explaining them in more detail and sharing some real life strategies you can deploy *Right Now* so you can achieve true success.

When you read through these Four Ps consider what success in these areas looks like to you. Who comes to mind when you think of a successful person? What qualities do they have? What do they do? What do they avoid?

Many people's answers to those questions will differ based on a number of factors, but one thing about success is true no matter what you see as success or who you consider successful.

The Success Equation

$$I + P + RA = \text{Success}$$

Every successful person achieved and maintains success by living their life consistent with one simple formula, which I call "The Success Equation." The Success Equation is equally simple and powerful. If you learn the Four Ps and live your life consistent with the Success Equation, your future will be unlimited. Here's what the formula stands for:

Intention + Presence + Repeated Action = Success

With this Success Equation, success can be whatever you want it to be. Want to lose weight? Intention, presence, and repeated actions focused on weight loss can get you there. Want to grow your business? Intention, presence, and repeated actions focused on business growth can get you there. It's that simple.

Intention is how you go about your activities. Are you going through the motions with your business, waiting for people to call you and hoping you'll make payroll? Or are you making the phone calls, sending the emails, and doing high-quality work that will make your clients sing your praises? Successful people spend each moment, activity, day, and week with great intention. They have a plan and goals for their personal and professional lives and make sure they speak and act with great intention to lead them closer to their goals.

Presence is your mindset and concentration in each moment. Being truly present in life helps you catch yourself before doing or saying something that's inconsistent with who you are and who you want to become. It also helps you identify times where you said or acted inconsistent with your vision of yourself and didn't catch yourself in the moment so you can make a better decision next time. Successful people are present. They are self-aware. This helps them avoid or minimize and learn from mistakes.

Repeated action is taking action enough times that it builds momentum and creates habit. Just like you can't go to the gym once and expect to walk out with six-pack abs, you can't achieve true success with small bursts of action. Success requires you to be intentional and present and take actions that lead you towards a successful life day in and day out for a long period of time. The most successful people are not overnight successes. Many work for months or years before anyone notices.

The Ultimate Success Stopper

I do have one warning for you, though. As powerful as the Success Equation is, there's one, big, potentially evil thing that's ten times more powerful than the Success Equation. It's the ultimate success stopper. I can't move on to explain the Four Ps in more detail without first warning you to be on the lookout for the success stopper, because the only way to defeat the success stopper is to be aware of it, so that when it creeps up, you know exactly what it is and can confidently push it aside.

I'm talking about your internal dialogue, your doubts, or limiting beliefs. This is a story that you tell yourself that usually starts with something like "I can't afford it" or "I've tried that before and it didn't work," or "I'm not that lucky," or "I have bad knees, so I can't exercise," or "But I . . ." or "Nobody would love me because . . ."

When I was starting out in business, I had a bad limiting belief: I kept telling myself if I built a team I would not be able to live the life I wanted because I would feel strange taking the vacation time I wanted or playing golf as much as I wanted. I was only able to stop that story from holding me back once I realized not building a team would keep me from achieving my goal of helping 100 million people change their lives. I knew I could not help so many people without a team.

Just like my story stopped me from achieving my larger goals, your story is the only thing that can stop you from achieving yours. All you need to do is act with intention, be present, repeat the necessary actions to achieve your goals, and don't let your story sabotage you. If you don't believe you can be healthy, you won't do the things you need to do to be healthy. If you don't believe you deserve to be loved, you won't find someone to love you. Is your story stopping you from achieving a life of your dreams?

You now have the solution to achieve success and the mindset to defeat success's greatest enemy, your story. Next let's go through the Four Ps so you can further develop the personal traits needed to achieve success and avoid sabotaging yourself on your path to greatness.

Psychology: Who You Are and How You Are Showing Up

For the purpose of this book, the focus of the psychology discussion is twofold. First, we will focus on training your mind. Second, we will briefly address the minds of others because you have much less control (think zero!) over other people's minds than your own.

To start, pull out one of the eulogies you drafted in Phase 1. Read through it again, and as you're doing so, circle two or three words that describe who you strive to be. Pick words you want to define you as a person. Of course there will be many more than three words that describe you, but for this exercise I want you to just choose three.

When I did this I circled these three words: Present, Intentional, and Joyful.

Once you have your three words it's time to ingrain these words into your mind, into your soul. These three words will start to define you. They will become more than just words. They will become your identity; they will become who you are. This is the most powerful part to this exercise so I hope you're ready.

Train Your Brain – The Seven-Day Experience

For the next seven days I want you to use your phone to help you train your brain to set you up for achieving success through your actions. To do this, you'll need to set alarms on your phone to ring every two or three hours between the time you wake up and when you go to sleep. In the note section of the alarm, which tells you what the alarm is about, insert your three words. Every two or three hours your phone will go off and you'll be reminded of your three words.

The alarm section of your phone should look something like mine, except with your words, of course:

When the alarm goes off, let it chime. Don't be so quick to switch it off. When you see your words, take ten seconds to ask yourself whether you've lived true to those three words since the last time the alarm

rang. For me it would be "Am I being present? Am I being intentional? Am I being joyful?" If not, "thank the alarm" for helping you out and adjust your behavior accordingly.

It may take you a few days to really get the hang of this. It may happen sooner, but the power and value lie in the repetition. I urge you to take this exercise on with full intention and I promise you're going to see massive positive change in your life. This seven-day experience lets you automate part of the Success Equation to help you stay present, live intentionally, and repeatedly ask yourself if you're living and acting consistent with your vision of success.

The purpose for the alarm is to help propel you to your true self. Surely three or four dings throughout a workday is a small price to pay. Even so, stick it on vibrate, strategically set the alarms so they won't go off in regularly scheduled meetings or another time you want to avoid. Or make your alarm tone the same as your ringtone, so you can look at your phone and "silence the call." Just don't give up before you even start. It's too important.

Personally, my alarms go off regardless of my circumstances. If I am in a meeting, an event, or lining up to take a swing on the golf course, they still go off. Why? Because I have made a decision to live a life of intention and presence. A shanked drive or a polite "excuse me" is a very small price to pay for the accountability the alarms provide. But that's just me.

After a week, you can adjust it down to three times per day and test yourself. Has your commitment to living your three words gotten worse? Test your awareness. Be conscious about how you're showing up. If you find you're defaulting back to bad habits, ramp it back up to five alarms per day, or more. I promise your life will never be the same.

But don't just take my word for it. A client of mine, Jessica, wrote that within one week of setting five alarms with the words "confident, engaged, and passionate," she became more present during daily interactions, felt better about herself, and increased her drive and passion to accomplish her goals.

The Next Level – Add Value to Others

If you're as serious as I am about living life on your own terms, here are a couple of ways you can take it to the next level.

The next time you talk on the phone or meet someone in person ask yourself this question:

What could I do *Right Now* that will ensure I am showing up as the person I desire to be?

And how can I make this person feel as though they are the only person on the planet and that they have my full attention?

Because one of my identifying words is joyful, I always enter a conversation with the goal of having more positive energy than the person I am about to engage with. This can make someone's day and, more importantly, help me live my life's true mission.

You know those people you just meet and it feels like you've been lifted to a new level and empowered? That's what I aim to achieve every single time I meet someone. Think of the power this type of thinking can have. I am deliberately going into a conversation with the full intention of empowering the person. I am not leaving it up to chance. I am engaging in deliberate and purposeful action.

What if one of your words is "inspiring?" How could you show up and inspire? How would you need to stand? How would you need to sound? What would you need to say and do? These are all important questions you must ask yourself regardless of the word you're trying to identify with. The key is we are not trying to enter into a situation as a person we are not; we are trying to enter a situation as the person we truly are at our core and who we are truly developing into. It may feel strange, or fake even, but remember, these words are who you dreamed you'd become and who you really believe you are deep down. The only difference is you're deciding to start being that person *Right Now* instead of waiting to become that person over time. Those concerns will go away as you see the power of this process.

To really take this to the next level, ask the person you just engaged with for feedback by asking if they felt you were being your words. I get it may be a bit creepy to ask the local barista if you were joyful or present, so it's probably best to start with people closest to you. I could ask my friends anything and know I couldn't come off any weirder than they already think I am, so there's nothing to lose and everything to gain. Feedback is rocket fuel for rapid growth. Sadly, so many people avoid asking for feedback because they are scared of getting their feelings hurt or having to face a reality they have been denying for too long.

Next Level Task: Ask someone who is important in your life for feedback about your three words. Do it *Right Now*. Let the person know you've chosen these three words and you'd like to ask them for their honest opinion and perhaps some accountability.

Insert your words below:

Reflection

What did you discover about your psychological self in this section? What was the number one thing that stood out to you?

What is the one thing you'll be doing differently in your life starting *Right Now?*

Take a minute to reflect on your answers to these questions and get ready to develop an ideal physiological you.

Physiology: Fine-Tuning Your Vessel

"Take care of your body, it is the only place you have to live."
—**Jim Rohn**

This section will help you let in, and keep, the positive inputs that move you towards your true physical self and push or keep out the bad inputs that get in your way. Before we get too deep into the materials, though, be sure you check with your doctor before trying any of the processes or techniques I discuss in this book. As you know by now, I am not a doctor, and I certainly don't know your unique physical needs or challenges. The information I am sharing here is informational, designed to get you thinking differently. Have a conversation with your doctor to help you achieve similar results in a way that works for your unique situation. The point of this is for you to start improving your physiological self—*Right Now.*

As with the mind, we are only gifted with one body, one vessel for success. It's up to us to ensure we make the most of it. We must fuel it, care for it, and, most importantly provide it with an environment in which it can flourish. We must learn to avoid what we already know is bad for us and create a maintainable and achievable process to ensure our vessel remains intact so we can excel. But we are not going to talk too much about the "big three" questions my health and wellness company has heard hundreds of thousands of times:

1. How do I lose fat?
2. How do I build muscle?
3. How do I have more energy?

Those questions are important, but they are only surface-level physical changes. If you'd like further resources and secrets to a leaner and more toned body, I have put some up on the resources page at http://brettcampbell.net/right-now-resources.

Instead, we are going to go much deeper and address two questions I have been obsessed with for many years:

1. How do I live longer?
2. How do I improve the quality of my life?

Those two questions are far more powerful than the best fat loss strategies, or lean muscle-building secrets. In fact, we are living during a time where there's exponential growth in life expectancy around the world. In the year 1 A.D., the average global life expectancy was twenty-six years. Eighteen hundred years later it had increased by only two years, to twenty-eight years old. In just over two hundred years since then, the average global life expectancy has lengthened to sixty-eight years. That includes infant deaths and places with poor water and resources. For those reading this book, it's highly likely you're going to far outlive those sixty-eight years. In the United States, for example, life expectancy is approaching eighty years, and with the advances in medical treatment and technology, many older people are aging with a very high standard of living. In fact, an entire team of scientists are currently working full-time to expand healthy life expectancy. Those scientists predict that they will be able to expand the healthy life expectancy to 130 years by the year 2045!

I don't know about you, but I want to far outlive the average life expectancy the statistics tell me I'll likely have. Wouldn't you love to add more quality years to your life? Of course you would, especially after you start living a life of your dreams.

So how do you maximize both the quality and quantity of years left? Most experts tell you to do some combination of eating three healthy meals a day, exercising regularly, and having regular sex. Unlike the so-called experts, I'm going to share three lifestyle changes that have the potential for being even more transformative for your quality of life and lifespan and strongly suggest you talk with your doctor about how these changes might help you, too.

I. Invest in Longer and Better Sleep
(seven to nine quality hours)

Quality sleep is the most underrated and overlooked aspect of living a strong, long, and healthy life.

The human body is designed to work off a natural physiological cycle of about twenty-four hours that persists even in the absence of external cues. This is known as the circadian rhythm. When the sun rises in the morning the hormone cortisol is released into your body to wake you up and prepare you for the day. In the afternoon, cortisol levels begin to drop and melatonin (another hormone), growth hormones, and repair hormones start releasing.

This is preparing you for sleep and repair on both the physical and mental levels. If we follow our natural sleep cycles and allow our bodies to do what they are supposed to do, we should be starting to wind down in the afternoon and be asleep by 10:00 p.m. Your body will make most physical repairs in the first four hours of sleep and then spend the time after 2:00 a.m. doing psychogenic, or mental, repair until you wake up. The cycle looks something like this:

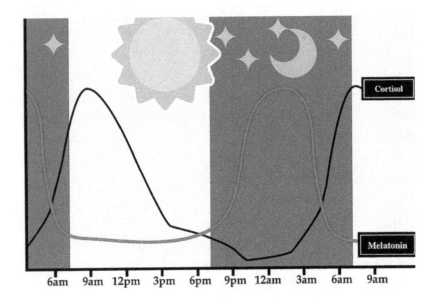

6am 9am 12pm 3pm 6pm 9pm 12am 3am 6am 9am

That's why the "four-hour sleeper" is on a path of destruction whether they know it or not. Their brain hardly gets any help at night. There's simply no healthy long-term alternative to consistent high-quality sleep. Show me a person who says they can operate on four hours of sleep, and I'll show you a person who is one night away from exhaustion and burnout! They may think they can operate off of four hours of sleep, but I assure you they are operating at a subpar level and nowhere near their true potential. Not only does science back this up, but I know firsthand because I was this person for a long time. I'd stay up all night working on my computer until almost midnight and be up in the morning at 4:00 a.m. to train clients. As you'll see in a moment, this practice is ridiculous and outright dangerous.

A disruptive sleep/wake cycle can also lead to adrenal fatigue. Chronic exposure to stress and light (including TV, phones, and computers) at night requires the adrenals to release more cortisol than normal and disrupts the natural cycle of melatonin and other hormones taking you to sleep. Excessive cortisol levels contribute to several health issues including chronic fatigue syndrome, viral, fungal, and bacterial infections, and headaches. Excess cortisol is also the number one contributor to belly fat storage. That's why it's very important to start paying attention to and respecting your natural circadian rhythm and allowing your adrenals to rest and recover.

Here are six tips to help you get more and better sleep:

1. Black out your room.
Get black-out curtains or put blankets over your windows to stop light from coming into your room. Don't let that streetlamp across the street or your neighbor's motion lights interfere with your quality of sleep. The darker the better. Studies have shown that even small lights disrupt your melatonin release, which you need to sleep, and your cortisol release continues instead.

2. Keep your phone out of your bedroom.
Most people wake up and immediately check social notifications, feeds, news, and entertainment stories late into the night and first thing in the morning. Their brain speeds until they fall asleep and then immediately jolts full speed from the moment they wake up. If they wake up in the middle of the night for some reason, they might even see and check a notification on their phone that keeps them up for an extra half hour or longer, further disrupting their physical and mental recovery. In fact, even the glow of your phone can disrupt much needed melatonin release. Avoid this by leaving your phone out of your bedroom.

Personally, I leave my phone downstairs, because I know if it's by me at night, it's far too easy to flip it open and check out the latest sports scores. If you use your phone for an alarm, get an alarm. They still make them.

3. Practice the art of gratitude (using the "Ten by Ten" Gratitude Method).

Before I allow myself to fall to sleep I tell myself ten things I am grateful for, saying them to myself and then elaborating on each of them in my head. This sets my mind up for a great night's sleep because when you're grateful for something, you can't be any other emotion. And before my feet touch the floor in the morning, I tell myself ten more things I am grateful for. I call this the "ten by ten" gratitude method. Shifting the first thing you do in the morning and the last thing you do before bed from checking Facebook, or watching TV, to listing ten things you're grateful for is a powerful way to start and end each day well.

Please note this exercise is supposed to be a comforting and a beautiful experience. Don't get stressed if you can't come up with ten things right away. It simply means you need to practice the art of gratitude. It will get easier, I promise.

4. Do not drink fluids too close to bedtime.

Limiting water intake prior to sleeping is a good way to make sure you're not waking up to pee at night. Find your sweet spot. For me, not drinking for an hour before bed and going to the bathroom before I get in bed does the trick.

5. Don't consume caffeine after lunchtime.

Caffeine has a half-life of up to six hours. So if you have a double shot of coffee at 3:00 p.m. you'll still have 75–150 milligrams (mg) of caffeine in your blood stream at 9:00 p.m. Six hours later, well into your psychogenic (mental) repair cycle of immune function, you'll still have 40–75 mg of caffeine stimulating your adrenal glands and producing cortisol.

6. Invest in a *great* bed.

I recently invested in a $15,000 bed. I get it, it's not for everyone. However if I am going to be spending a full third of my life in bed (and a very important third) then I better make the most of it. My bed allows me to sleep in zero gravity; it's adjustable and puts me into a position of weightlessness. It takes all pressure off of my joints and muscles and allows for optimum blood flow. It sets me up for the best recovery and repair possible. It has a fifteen-minute massage setting that prepares my body for rest, and 95 percent of the time I am fast asleep before it even stops.

You may not be interested in spending so much on a bed, and that's fine. I wasn't too keen on it either at first. I was used to sleeping on a bed that cost less than $2,000, and I thought that was high end. On the other hand, most people are happy to spend over $15,000 on a car in which they may only spend thirty to sixty minutes per day. But what about the place you're spending a third of your life? I'll leave that question with you. If I had to make the choice, I'd rather drive a $2,000 car and sleep in the $15,000 bed than the other way around. The point is you need a quality mattress for quality sleep.

Once you fully grasp that sleep is your friend and not your foe, you'll open your life up to a newfound sense of energy. Start implementing some of these suggestions and you'll start to see dramatic changes. In fact, Anna, who I told you about in the beginning of the book, told me that even "small changes" in her bedroom helped her go from five to eight hours of sleep a night and, in her words, she has "never felt better."

A special bonus, as you increase the quality of your sleep, you'll also automatically start to lose body fat and build lean muscle. That's right, less fat and more muscle, just as a byproduct of getting a good night's rest. That's what I call a triple whammy!

II. Drink Your Veggies

Vegetables are full of so many health benefits I could fill an entire book with why you need to eat your veggies. Despite that, the vast majority of adults don't eat enough vegetables. In fact, the Australian Health Survey of 2011, conducted by the Australian Bureau of Statistics, concluded that over 90 percent of adults had an inadequate vegetable intake.

I don't know about you, but I have never been able to physically eat enough vegetables. If I had to literally eat all the vegetables I consumed, I would likely not eat nearly enough vegetables either. As a kid, I would eat all my vegetables first, simply to get rid of them so I could enjoy the protein, my favorite part of dinner.

That's why the best purchase we have ever made for our kitchen is a juicer. Here are five real-world reasons why I believe you should be drinking your vegetables, too.

1. Raw vegetables have more healthy enzymes than cooked ones.

In the book *How to Eat, Move, and Be Healthy*, world-renowned nutrition expert Paul Check, advocates eating your vegetables raw because the process of cooking kills enzymes that are needed to aid in digestion, which generally can't survive in temperatures beyond 118 degrees Fahrenheit. Juicing, then, is an excellent way to get nutrients from your raw veggies and fruits without having to eat a barrel full of food. Because many of the essential nutrients in fruits and vegetables oxidize very rapidly upon juicing, be sure to drink your juices immediately after making them. Making juice and leaving it in the fridge for a while will basically leave you with sugar water.

2. Juicing is convenient.

In less than five minutes I can create a tasty and nutritious vegetable juice containing all the nutrients needed for human optimization.

3. Juicing ensures you get all the veggies you need.

By juicing my vegetables I ensure I am consuming an adequate amount. This way I do not become one of the 90 percent of people who are not getting their basic requirements.

4. Juicing is an easy way to ensure variety.

Different plants provide different nutrients. By consuming a wide variety of nutrients you'll not only be doing your body a world of good, you'll also decrease your chances of acquiring food intolerances. Quick tip: The darker the color of the vegetable, the more likely it is to provide you with lots of great antioxidants, so be sure to mix in some dark ones.

5. Juicing is a personal lifestyle enhancer.

Juicing vegetables is the most efficient way to integrate a top, natural health enhancer into your daily routine. In addition to the health benefits, it adds time to my day while ensuring I consume the nutrients and antioxidants my body requires. I also don't enjoy sitting down and having to consume handfuls of spinach leaves. It makes me feel like a goat. I would much prefer putting them in a juicer along with a bunch of other vegetables and consume them that way. I now have vegetable smoothies for breakfast, lunch, and dinner, along with a form of protein for each meal.

I consume more vitamins and minerals than I ever have before, and in the first two weeks of switching to this style of eating (or in this case drinking) I lost eleven pounds of body fat. I can't guarantee you'll lose weight, too, but it was my experience and a great byproduct of this health shift.

Here's the recipe for my Go-To Green Smoothie, which serves two, so you can juice with a friend!

Big handful of spinach leaves (precise, I know)
1 cup of broccoli
Handful of green beans
1 carrot
½ standard size zucchini
1 cm squared piece of ginger (optional based on taste)
½ avocado
½ cucumber
500 ml of chilled purified water (this is the size of your standard 16.9 ounce water bottle)

You can add ½ apple or orange to bring up the taste levels, however I am happy to forgo a little taste for all the other amazing benefits.

Here's a sample day of my nutritional consumption:
Breakfast: Green smoothie with salmon or egg omelet
Lunch: Green smoothie with lean beef sausages, steak, chicken, or another source of protein
Dinner: Same as lunch.

If you want to get your hands on a ton of clean eating recipes be sure to visit our resource page http://brettcampbell.net/right-now-resources. Whatever method you prefer. My message here is to ensure you're consuming your vegetables. Don't make me tell your mother on you.

Too many people think good nutrition is far more complex than it is. I have been in the health and wellness space for years, and it even gets confusing for me at times. One expert will say one thing and another says the opposite. Keep it simple. Test a few things. Talk with your doctor or other local professional and see what works best for you.

III. Get Off Your Butt and Move a Little

We all know movement is essential for optimum health. Way too many people suffer health problems because they sit still all day, most of them in a chair all day at work. But movement doesn't have to involve driving to a gym, running on a treadmill, cardio kickboxing, or lifting weights. In this section I'll give you several simple yet very effective movement and exercise strategies you can implement into your life to improve your health.

Here are three practical alternatives to consider. You're unlikely to see the following recommendations in the generic world of exercise and movement. But they are just as, if not more, important than whatever type of exercise program you find on late night TV.

1. The 60x60x8 Reset Routine

This routine involves you moving for sixty seconds, every sixty minutes, for eight hours per day. Wherever you are and whatever you're doing, every sixty minutes get up and move for at least sixty seconds. Set more alarms on your phone to remind you if you have to. If you're on the computer working and you're sitting at a desk, then this is even more important. If you're already moving when the alarm goes off, that's great. Simply become aware that you're moving and give yourself a pat on the back.

In my routine I use a very similar process each time, although you can change it up if you like. I do a couple of tai chi movements where I simply swing my arms and rotate my torso. This helps release any stress I may be feeling in my arms and shoulders. Pick what works for you and go with it. It may be a couple of key stretches, a few push-ups or jumping jacks, or whatever else works for you. Just move. The stimulation caused by this short sixty-second effort will take your energy and mood to the next level. Test it and see.

If you're an employer or manager at work, consider adopting this principle with your team. I have taught this process to many corporate organizations and they love it. Not only will it increase productivity, it will bring an element of fun and self-improvement to the entire workplace.

Plan your sixty-second movement right here so you can just get up and do it by writing out the movements you'll do below:

2. 4x4 Awareness of Breath Routine

This routine can be done at any time, although I tie it into the end of my 60x60x8 resets in an effort to maximize efficiency. Once I finish moving for sixty seconds, I move through this process. It's a very calming exercise that ensures any tension I have been carrying around for the last hour totally dissipates. It allows me to do a master reset, just like you would by holding down the power button on your computer until it powers down.

For this exercise place one hand on your stomach and the other hand on your chest. Breathe in for four seconds through your nose and into your stomach (this is called diaphragm breathing). You'll notice the hand on your stomach rises while the hand on your chest doesn't move. Breathe out through your mouth for four seconds, shying (moaning), as you release the breath. If you're in a crowded place, feel free to make a whisper sound or find a place where you can be alone for thirty seconds or so. Do this five or six times. If my day is a little more stressful, I aim for ten or more. This thirty to eighty seconds is so therapeutic and beneficial. You simply must try it, *Right Now* in fact. Then come back and keep reading. I guarantee you'll have more energy and greater clarity for the rest of the material. Imagine having more energy, greater clarity, and more self-awareness all day!

Well now you can by implementing these little, focused pauses into your day.

3. Forced Movement

Forced movement is different than the 60x60x8 reset routine in that it's more of a lifestyle change than a set hourly routine. Unfortunately for many people, forced movement is a rare habit. I became very aware of this concept when I was starting my business because it was very common for me to sit at my computer for eight to ten hours straight without getting out of the seat. Can you relate at all?

This was physically and emotionally crippling. I thought because I was spending so much time at my desk working I was getting more done and progressing faster in life. But the reality was the opposite, which you'll hear more about when we look into productivity in the coming pages.

Those long periods of sitting got so out of control I got to a point where I had to implement forced movement. For me, it involved committing to going on daily walks with my wife and our two pugs and committing to the gym with a friend and accountability partner. Now I add as much forced movement into my life as possible, like my twice-per-week golf games and walking the course instead of using a cart.

Here are four simple and effective forced movement strategies you could implement immediately that require very little extra effort.

- Park your car in the farthest away parking space. Those extra hundred steps each day will add up fast.
- Take the stairs for anything under five levels (then sneak up to six, seven, or more). *Remember to check with your doctor first if you have any health conditions.
- Alternate between sitting and standing desk setups. (This helps lengthen your back and can help prevent lower back problems.)

- Create a light stretching routine in the shower (I have five stretch poses I run through twice a day in the shower. This really helps with my mobility.)

What daily forced movements will you add into your life?

Personal Knowledge Development: The Most Valuable Asset You'll Ever Acquire!

The third component of developing your "self" in the Develop Phase of the *Right Now* framework involves acquiring personal (and practical) knowledge. This section gives you an effective and efficient way to do so.

When I left school and became a cabinetmaker, I had no idea how to build a kitchen, wooden stairs, or windows. The only woodworking skills I had were from high school where I learned how to build a pencil case and boomerang. Yet in less than three years I was not only one of the fastest and best kitchen builders in the factory, I had also acquired the skills to build my very first home.

As I identified more and more goals that required new skills and knowledge, I got very intentional with developing skill after skill. I call this the "Apprentice Method," which follows a "give, watch, learn, and become" pattern for skill acquisition.

It all started on my very first day as a cabinetmaker. I had no idea what I was doing, so I asked my boss, "Who is the best kitchen maker in the factory?" He pointed to a guy called Baz. "Baz," he said, "is our best tradesman. But he doesn't like apprentices, so if you want to learn you should look to learn from one of the other guys," suggesting a couple others who would be willing to help me.

As an apprentice, your first title might as well be "Broomstick Technician" because your primary role is sweeping up and removing all the sawdust and offcuts of timber, along with any other messes the tradesmen make. As you can imagine, that's not too much fun. I quickly realized the sooner I learned to build a kitchen, the sooner I would get to stop picking up after other people and transition into having someone clean up after me. I also knew Baz was the key to making that transition happen faster.

I made it my mission to change Baz's perception about apprentices, or at least his perception about having me as an apprentice. So every day I asked Baz if he had anything I could help him with. Every day he said no. So, every day, I would find jobs close to where Baz worked so I could watch him work and he could watch me hustle. He really was miles ahead of everyone else.

After a while, I started to feel like my days were stuck on repeat. I would sweep, clean, and watch Baz. I would pester him to the point he told me to get out, on multiple occasions. The next day I would start again: sweep, clean, pester, sweep, clean, pester.

After what seemed like hundreds of those same days I became pretty frustrated, so I went up to him and said "I've asked you every day if you want help or if you have anything for me to do. Why do you keep saying no?" A question born out of frustration turned out to be exactly a turning point in developing the relationship that would help me quickly become one of the best cabinetmakers around. Baz shared that he never liked apprentices because too many had screwed up the work and he hated having to start over or fix their mistakes. In other words, he might not be opposed to the teaching side of an apprenticeship relationship. He just didn't want them to make more work for him. I had my opening. He knew I was different than others because I was the only one to keep on him for so long and to ask about his concerns.

It didn't take long for things to change. "Brett!" I heard, as I swept up the factory. "Get your arse over here!" It was Baz. I ran over. He was standing next to a trolley full of timber and got right to his point. "Alright, you can make my drawers, but if you mess it up I'm not letting you do it again."

It was my chance. "I won't mess it up, Baz. I promise. I have been practicing with scraps and I know what I am doing." Away I went to prove myself. I figured I had watched him do this hundreds of times so I knew exactly what he wanted me to do. I knew his method. Four hours later, I wheeled the trolley back to Baz with twenty completed drawers ready to be installed into the kitchen.

"Not bad, boy," Baz growled. "What do you think? You reckon you could make this as well?" He pointed to a cabinet with a couple of shelves in it. "Sure I can," I replied, although I had never done such a thing before. "Okay, away you go. I want them done by tonight," he instructed. And off I went again.

At that point I wasn't yet one of the best. But I had worked hard, watched the best, offered help over and over again, and even practiced in private. When I wasn't sweeping the floor or pestering Baz, I was getting ready for showtime. I went outside where all the offcuts and scraps of wood would be thrown away to practice connecting pieces of wood, making sure everything was flush and square. I was preparing for the time I would be given the opportunity to put a real cabinet together, making sure that first time would not be the last.

I was ready to become one of the best cabinetmakers around. By continuing to do the same, giving, watching, and learning, over and over, I quickly became Baz's right-hand man. He said jump, and I'd ask how high and where he would like me to land. I soaked up everything I could for the opportunity to be with, and learn from, the best.

That, my friend, was the beginning of my Give, Watch, Learn, and Become method of skill acquisition. Here are four key takeaways about this method I want to highlight to help you master any skill you need or want to acquire.

I. Quality Knowledge Acquisition Is Built Right In

I acquired the knowledge first by watching, listening, and doing test runs with scrap pieces of timber, all while I was waiting for my chance. Other apprentices threw those timber scraps away to be burned. I was never told to practice with the scraps, and I don't even think our boss would have approved it because he probably would have been more concerned about the screws I was wasting. Yet after all that practice I ended up becoming the first apprentice in factory history to complete a four-year apprenticeship in three years.

Apply this component to your path to your best life:

What skills must you acquire to achieve the outcomes you desire?

What habits must you adopt in order to achieve the outcomes you desire?

Who can you learn from?

How can you start practicing *Right Now*?

II. Become the Apprentice No Matter What Stage of Life You're In

Obviously I was an actual, formal apprentice. But there have been many other times when I adopted the apprentice mindset to learn a new skill. When I first became a fitness professional, I studied from the best I could find. When I first became a business and life coach, I learned from the best of the best.

I quickly learned to embrace that there's always a first time. No matter how successful you are in life, if you've never done something before, you're the apprentice. That's okay. Never be afraid to be the apprentice. Never be afraid to find people who are further along than you in a particular area and learn from them. I get such a rush being around people who are smarter or more skilled than me. It tells me I am about to learn a ton, and that there's a wealth of knowledge there for me to soak up. Help people who are doing what you want to do. Tell them you want to help and learn from them. Ask how you can help more and more. Give, give, and give some more.

III. Seek Out the Best and Prove Yourself

Baz was not the easiest guy to impress, to say the least, so it was an uphill battle from the start. But I wasn't going to budge. I said I would prove myself by doing the hard work and letting my skills and enthusiasm do the talking. And I didn't give up, actually becoming really good friends with Baz along the way. Fortunately for you, Baz is the exception. Most of the time, the most successful people are also the most generous, as it's a rare exception that someone rises to the top without being generous.

When I discovered the Internet was going to be my primary vehicle to connect with customers, I did the exact same thing. I sought out the best in the industry. I did everything I could to add value to them and soak up as much as I could along the way. I jumped on planes and traveled halfway around the world to learn from the best.

When I wanted to become a speaker, I adopted the apprentice attitude again. I approached one of the best and asked how I could add value to him. I went to every event his team ran. I bought my own plane tickets and followed him around. I proved I was serious and willing to put in the hard work. After a few events I asked if I could introduce him from the stage, pump up the crowd, and then call him to the stage to work his magic. After a few times, he finally said yes!

I can still remember the night before the event. I literally had ten lines I needed to deliver. I practiced and practiced those ten lines until I felt like I could deliver them in my sleep. I was so pumped up walking to the stage that day. I was in the zone. I was about to kill it. A few lines later my mentor walked on stage and I walked off, sitting down at the back of the room. It was incredible, and all because I sought out the best and proved myself.

IV. Never Give Up!

There I was, sitting in the back of the room feeling like a superhero, all pumped up after introducing my mentor from the very stage he would perform on. I was on top of the world. I couldn't wait for the day to end so I could ask my mentor what he thought of my introduction. I was very open to feedback because I was so hungry to learn. But I knew I crushed it!

The moment finally came. "Your delivery was great," he started. But then he continued. "Well, the words you said came out great anyway." "What do you mean?" I asked. "You forgot 80 percent of what you were supposed to say," he replied.

My heart sank. I blew it. I had ten lines, but apparently I only said two of them. I guess I was a bit too excited and had a brain explosion on stage. I was gutted, demoralized. After all that hard work, I finally got a chance and screwed it up.

At that moment I could have either given up or learned and moved forward. Many people would have given up, and that's why many people aren't living a life of their dreams. But I knew speaking was going to play a massive role in my overall life mission, so I was not about to give up over one screwup, so I doubled down, learned, and moved forward.

I practiced and practiced, served and observed. My mentor took notice of my continued hard work and refusal to give up. He saw the improvements I had made and rewarded me with another chance. That time, I left no stone unturned and delivered the best opening I could hope for. The crowd was pumped, I was pumped, and my mentor was pumped.

In fact, he was so pumped he asked me to run my own sessions. Of course I said yes! Sessions led to leading days. And the days led to multiday workshops all by myself. None of that would have happened if I had given up after that first disaster.

Now let's apply this to you. What do you want to do? What do you want to become? Who is doing that well *Right Now*? What do you need to learn? Where can you learn that? Answer those questions and you'll know exactly where to go next. There has never been an easier time to learn and consume content. You can learn a new language using an app on your phone. You can watch a five-minute YouTube video and learn how to cut someone's hair (but please don't . . .). There's Wi-Fi on airplanes. You can buy a course with hours of organized and top-quality information from experts these days. There are so many places to learn from the best.

But another caution: The major problem today is not lack of information, but rather information overload. Information overload may be the single most dangerous factor holding people back once they decide where they want to go. Some people spend years learning and learning and never start doing.

I'm here to encourage you to start doing something—*Right Now*—by taking even little steps forward. Start small and grow big.

Here are some practical and useful tips to get information to help you learn faster than you ever thought possible while avoiding information overload.

1. Find your best one or two methods of information consumption and stick to those.

Yes, you need to get information and I don't care how you get it. Books, audio books, podcasts, YouTube videos, live events, informal mentoring, hiring a coach or formal mentor, whatever. It doesn't matter. Just don't do it *all*. You'll get information overload.

2. Learn in chunks.

My sweet spot is one hour of audio or, if I am reading a physical book, about twenty to thirty written pages at a time. Any more and I'll start to forget what I was listening to or reading. Find your sweet spot and don't fight it. It will grow over time, but if you consume too much you won't comprehend much of it.

My mission with this book is to provide you with actionable and useful strategies you can implement in small chunks. That's why I stop you at times and ask you to complete an exercise or two. I know by practicing and going through the process in chunks, it will help you retain and apply the information.

A client of mine, Keith, came to me to help him grow his business. Keith is a rock star in the business world, full of potential, but was struggling with information (and direction) overload. He felt stuck. I could see right away Keith needed to do less in order to accomplish more. I encouraged him to step back, identify his goals, and then break down those goals into small steps, learning in small chunks and then taking small, but deliberate steps forward. Through that new mindset, Keith reenergized his personal life and business and started knocking out his goals like never before. You'll likely find you also get more done in less time by learning—and doing—in small chunks.

3. Follow only a couple of key experts in a field at a time.

Imagine receiving relationship advice from five different relationship coaches or learning how to build wealth from five different financial advisors. One of two things would happen in those situations. Either they all tell you the same thing, and you just wasted four-fifths of your money, or they all tell you different things and you have no idea what you really should do. It's just not practical.

So why do so many people do this with skills? If you want to learn how to eat healthy, find one or two professionals who you connect with and stick with them. Only take advice from people who have actually been successful building what you're looking to build. Everything I share in here, I have done successfully. I have experimented firsthand and discovered through the school of hard knocks what works and what doesn't. Be wary of so-called "experts" who are only experts in teaching and not doing.

4. Stop only consuming information and start doing.

I don't care how much you know, how many books you've read, or how many seminars you've attended. I only care about how much you do and how many people you've helped with what you've learned. You can have walls full of self-help, business training, or diet books, but if you haven't actually done anything with this information, what have you really accomplished?

What action did you implement into your life from the last book you read? What effect did the last seminar have on your life? I hope you can come up with something. I know you can come up with something based on what you're reading here if you go through the eulogies, questions, and exercises to take action!

But here's the tough question. Go to your bookshelf and pick up a book you read over a year ago. Pick an action you remember implementing from that book when you read it, but for some reason are no longer doing. Why aren't you doing it? Was it not working? Was it a choice? Or did life get in the way? Did you let life outmaneuver your brain, your willpower? Or did you jump at the next "expert" or "five-step plan"?

Too many people let life get in the way and, when the excitement of the information consumption wears off, move onto the next book, video, or seminar, and so on and so on. Too much knowledge and not enough action will cause you to travel off path and spin in circles. Your bookshelf turns into an information mecca of hopes and dreams and that's how it remains.

Keep the ratio of "learning to doing" to a manageable level or you'll end up doing nothing. And please wait to read the next book on the shelf until you've implemented and gotten results from the one you're reading *Right Now*. Deal? Knowledge may be powerful, but application of knowledge is where the real magic happens.

Maybe it's time to purge some of that content that's piling up around you. I recently convinced a friend to get rid of 90 percent of the materials he had accumulated in his office. He had a huge collection of books, courses, and other learning material, much of which was unopened. Instead of being inspired by his collection, he became deflated and often overwhelmed because he could see all the materials he had never opened and books he had read but not applied. He saw broken promises to himself and thousands of dollars in sunk costs sitting on shelves gathering dust.

Removing the materials was a tough experience for him, but the next time I visited his office it was transformational. The shelves were clear and uncluttered. The energy in the room was electric. I could see in his face the weight of disappointment was lifted off of his shoulders. The distraction was gone.

I am in no way, shape, or form suggesting you stop learning entirely. But I *am* suggesting you focus more on *applying* the knowledge than you do on *acquiring* it. Even better, maybe try learning by doing, like I did that day when I bombed on stage or when I practiced on the scraps after watching Baz work. Try my Apprentice Method. Start giving to someone who has the skills you want to acquire. Watch how they work, the tools they use, the care they put into their craft. Learn from what they do. Ask questions if you can. Practice as much as you can. "Giving, watching, and learning" will help you get noticed and acquire the skills needed to become what you want to be.

Productivity: Getting More Done in Less Time

You're in an incredibly exciting place. You've discovered your true self, designed your life, and begun mastering your mind and body to set yourself up for extraordinary success. Now you're about to learn some incredible and practical ways to pour gas on the fire you've lit inside you to get much more done in a lot less time!

The first step in getting more done in less time is to see time differently.

What if you didn't get paid in dollars anymore? What if you got paid in time? The more you did, the more time on Earth you had. Sounds crazy, right? Well leave it to the creative folks in Hollywood to come up with a concept and take it to an extreme, because that's exactly what was portrayed in the Justin Timberlake movie *In Time*.

In the movie, each person had a digital clock embedded on their arms that told them how long they had left to live, assuming they died of natural causes. To get more time, they needed to either do more to earn more, or steal it from others. If you didn't go to work or steal you would run out of time.

Time was also their method of payment. If you wanted to buy an ice cream, it would cost you some time. A meal would cost you time. If you spent too much, you would run out of time and die.

Imagine looking at your wrist and seeing how long you have left to live, knowing when your timer hit zero, you'd literally drop dead wherever you were. What a scary place to live, right? Because we don't have a timer on our wrists, we don't have that obvious reminder the characters in the movie did. Imagine looking at your wrist and seeing that you only had five years to live if you continued doing the same things you currently do? Would that be enough to force you into action?

There's a little bit of reality in the movie's premise, though. We *can* extend our lives by doing healthy things. And we can shorten it by doing things like sitting on the couch and eating pie all day, for example. So even as I bring you back to the real world, keep that concept close by. We might not have a clock in our wrists, but we do know time is limited and can be improved or extended through our actions. We do know time is the most valuable and limited resource on Earth. We do know it's the only resource on the planet everyone shares equally, on a day-to-day basis at least. Everyone gets twenty-four hours every day. The difference among people is what they do with that time. What we decide to do, how we decide to feel, and with whom we decide to spend that limited time, will determine the overall quality, impact, and meaning of our lives.

If you follow my suggestion, eight of those hours will be spent sleeping. If you have a typical nine to five job, another eight hours will be spent at work. That leaves eight hours each day for you to utilize in the best way possible.

As you can see in this graph representing the average number of minutes spent watching TV by country in 2013, the average American watched 293 minutes of TV per day, or almost five hours. People from China and Sweden watched 159 minutes per day, or a little over two-and-a-half hours. That's anywhere from one-third to over 60 percent of your nonworking awake time on the couch watching TV, and that

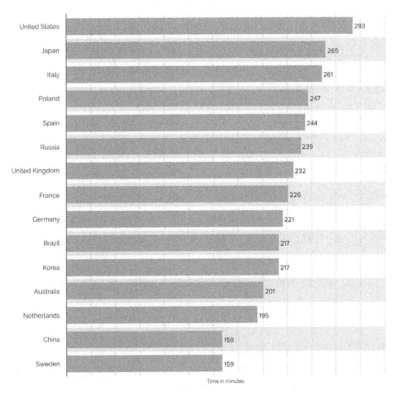

United States	293
Japan	265
Italy	261
Poland	247
Spain	244
Russia	239
United Kingdom	232
France	226
Germany	221
Brazil	217
Korea	217
Australia	201
Netherlands	195
China	159
Sweden	159

Time in minutes

doesn't even take commute time or getting ready in the morning into account. If you subtract the average commute and morning routine, the average person uses up quite a bit of their free time watching other people's lives on a screen instead of working on making their own lives the best they can be.

How are you spending the limited, precious minutes you have available each day? Are you adding value to your life? Or are you letting time pass by, sitting in front of a screen? With whom are you spending those minutes? Are they with people who lift you up, optimistic people who motivate you and inspire greatness? Or are you spending time listening to gossip or complaining?

The answers to these questions are critical. With only eight hours to work with, cutting out even one thirty-minute show and replacing it with some of the things we have talked about already can have a huge impact on your life.

But productivity doesn't only apply to how much work you get done or how much TV you watch in a day. It's far more than that. Productivity is about the quality and efficiency with which you engage or relate with each part of your life. Productivity is about both the quality and quantity of time we spend doing things we love or with people we love. It's about maximizing the impact of time.

Here are five of my favorite ways to maximize impact. Work these into your routine and you'll begin to feel like you have superpowers.

Five Extremely Powerful Productivity Tips for Maximum Impact

Productivity is just like any other skill. Your effectiveness will improve as you become more aware, practice, and work at it. That said, here are the five tips you can implement—*Right Now*—to start maximizing the impact of your time.

1. Become aware of how you spend your time.

You've seen this theme throughout. Step one is almost always becoming aware. Phase 1 in the *Right Now* framework is Discovery, for example. And we talked quite a bit about being aware of our surroundings and our thoughts in connection with the Develop Phase.

The same is true for productivity. Next time you sit down to watch some TV or surf the web ask yourself if that activity is going to serve you well. Is it adding to the quality of your life in a meaningful way, or is it an escape from something? Are you just procrastinating? Is there something else you could be doing instead that would help you more? Are you hiding from something by doing this instead?

Spend the next few minutes playing the last seven days in your head. What three things did you do during that time that you can cut down on (or out) to become more productive?

1.
2.
3.

2. Always have your phone on silent.

I very rarely get phone calls these days, simply because I have set my business and life up that way. But when I do, I answer one out of one hundred, mostly because I don't see or hear the phone ringing.

My phone is always on silent with the only noises I hear being the alarms I set to remind me of who I am and to do my 60x60x8 routine. It's one of the best things I have introduced into my life. What was often a distraction is now a supportive tool for me. It sits quiet until it's time to push me forward with my life plan.

At first I worried about missing calls, but have come to realize if it's important the person will leave a message. There's just no substitute for designing my life—phone included—by my agenda, preferred timing, and priorities and not someone else's. So it remains silent until looking at my phone fits within my schedule.

The effects go far beyond limiting interruptions, too. Consider this: I am currently writing a process for you to use to design and build a life that helps you become your true self. If I had my phone ringer on, it would be like having a time bomb sitting next to me waiting to go off. No matter how many times I have worked through the *Right Now* framework myself or with others, sitting next to a fully charged distraction device would both take away some creative juices and delay my ability to get this valuable information to people and help them start living the lives they deserve.

On top of that, the last thing I need is a telemarketer interrupting me to try and rent me new solar panels or give me bad investment advice. Instead, I am 100 percent focused on what I am writing, pumping out two thousand words an hour.

If my ability to write this book was diminished by constant interruptions, the people reading it—you—would get less direction, less production, and less support. I know, having gone through the process in my own life, the more productive I am in living my true purpose, the more people I can help. The more people I can help, the more people they can help. I don't just help people. I help people help people. That's the compound effect of productivity.

If the idea of silencing your phone all day makes you break into a cold sweat, start with keeping it silent when you're with others, especially your family. Add one hour a day until it's silent all day. I understand the urge of parents to keep their phones on in case of emergencies. But consider these two things. First, I don't know about you, but when I went to school, my mother didn't have a cell phone. In fact, we never even had a home phone. People had to call my grandmother's house and leave a message for us over there and I would literally run over to my grandmother's every day to collect our messages. The point is everything worked out just fine. I'm sure having your phone on silent will work out just fine for you, too.

Second, if you're not convinced, maybe this will help. Many phones now have a "do not disturb" function that allows you to have everything shut down but still let certain people through and allows people to get through if they hang up and call back right away, which indicates it's an emergency. Only then will you have to manually look at the phone and decide whether you'll answer. Add the kids' school numbers and closest relatives to the bypass list and stick your phone on do not disturb to start out.

3. Use a planning tool that works for you.

Everyone has a planning tool. Some people have a piece of paper. Others have an elaborate online/offline "system." Still others have sticky-note wallpaper. I have a planner. At first I used other people's planners, which was a great way to get started. But once I saw the power of the *Right Now* framework, I sat and created my own planner, which I called the *Right Now Daily Planner*™. (Creative name, I know . . . .)

The reason I created the *Right Now Daily Planner*™ is because using a generic planner worked for a while to start out with, but once I had my plan, using other planners felt like I was wearing someone else's shoes. I needed a planner that focused on the same things I was committed to.

Feel free to try it out yourself. I feel so strongly about connecting you with this plan that I have put an entire video training and sample pages you can print and try out for free right on the resources page at http://brettcampbell.net/right-now-resources.

There's even a free seven-day challenge for you to use the *Right Now Daily Planner*™ pages to make the next week your most productive week yet. Once you see the positive and meaningful results you can get in such a short period of time, you'll be hooked! If you don't connect with the *Right Now Daily Planner*™, don't force it. Give it a week and move on to something else until you find a planning system that works for you. That's the key. Find what works for your unique personality and tendencies and stick with it.

4. Stop "multitasking."

"Multitasking" is in quotes because "multitasking" is a myth. It's the rainbow-colored unicorn of the business world.

If you think you can read your email while filing your taxes and helping your kids with their homework you'll probably end up putting your income on your kid's homework and math problems on your taxes that you email to the wrong person. The point is, can you multitask? Yes. Should you multitask? No.

In fact, research conducted at Stanford University confirms people who are regularly bombarded with several streams of electronic information can't pay attention, recall information, or switch from one job to another as well as those who complete one task at a time. Researchers also say even trying to multitask may impair cognitive control. That's right. Finish your phone call, then type the text, then answer the email, and you'll still have time left over to give yourself a pat on the back. On top of that, the quality of your communications will be better too. Now *that's* a win!

Take a moment and think about all of the things you're doing right now. Obviously, you're reading, but chances are you may also be doing other things. Are you listening to music? Is the game on in the background? Is dinner on the stove?

Study after study has confirmed shifting between tasks reduces productivity because your brain must stop the first activity, start the other, and then get up to speed. Shifting back and forth over and over again—or "multitasking"causes your brain to stop and restart over and over again. It's like driving a car and steering left and right as you switch between slamming on the gas and slamming on the brakes. You'll move all over the place, but you won't get very far, and you'll end up crashing sooner or later.

Please stop "multitasking." You'll do more, and be more, by focusing on one task at a time and then moving to the next.

5. Take planned short and regular breaks.

Time your activities so they are completed quickly, in small chunks, and then take a brain break before starting the next one. Use the 60x60x8 reset routine in between tasks to recalibrate and refocus for the next burst of effort. Set small goals for each sixty-minute period then assess your effort and achievements. If any adjustments need to be made, adjust right away and get back on track.

Take a moment to celebrate. You just completed an extraordinarily powerful personal development lesson that will strengthen your mind, body, and routine so you can achieve your biggest goals faster than you could ever imagine.

CHAPTER 11

Develop Your Support

In his psychological theory *The Hierarchy of Needs*, Abraham Maslow concludes all people need to feel loved and that they belong. In this part of the *Right Now* framework we address those needs by helping you develop a strong support network to protect yourself and your goals.

This part of the Develop Phase will help you develop support from individuals, your community, automation, and technology. While each of those categories will mean something different to each person, the information I provide will make sure you feel love and belonging as you achieve your true life purpose. That feeling will keep you motivated, help you feel whole, and push you forward through the bumps and bruises. Let's dive in by first helping you form an individual support crew.

Your Individual Support Crew

Who are the key people in your life who you currently go to for support, help, guidance, and advice? Having supportive, optimistic people in your life is critical for personal improvement and accomplishment. It must be more than one person, too, because there's no one-size-fits-all supporter. You need a crew of individuals who have experience in different subject matter and whose opinions you trust on things like relationships, health, business, etc.

That subject matter distinction is important. If you look for support from someone in a subject matter that doesn't fit their experience, influence, or skill set, it can make you feel frustrated. It can also make you feel like you don't have support around you when you really do.

When that happens, it may be an issue of not finding the right person, and you quickly find that they don't share your vision or understand your struggles or concerns. In other words, sometimes you pick the wrong person for the right reasons.

Take my mother, for example. My mother is a valuable member of my individual support crew. She has provided immeasurable protection and support throughout my life. She is a source of love and advice in several important areas. But when it comes to real estate and home construction, I seek out other members of my individual support crew, especially since the whole "goat track" incident. Let me explain.

When I bought the land on which I was about to build my first house as a nineteen-year-old, I was excited to show my mother. Eager to see my mother's first reaction, I asked her to shut her eyes until I parked across the street and positioned the car so she could look up and be delighted.

"Open your eyes, Mom," I said, and she did. I expected her to be thrilled, but the first words out of her mouth were "Oh no, son! You bought a bloody goat track! How are you going to build a house up there?"

What she saw was a lot on a hill, covered in bushes and wildly overgrown grass—the only missing element being an actual goat. What I saw was a house, a front yard, and window boxes overflowing with flowers. All she could see was the present. All I could see was the future.

I was terribly disappointed with her response. I had hustled to buy that "goat track." I used every cent I had saved and thought I was making a wise investment, especially after having experienced the instability of motor home living.

My mother saw a "goat track," but I saw the future.

My mother wasn't the right fit in my "support crew" for this particular area. It wasn't her fault. Even though she loved me unconditionally, real estate wasn't her strong suit. Fortunately, my timing worked to my advantage. If I had taken my mother to the land before I bought it, I may not have gone through with the purchase, and it could have stopped me from making a decision that paid dividends for years to come.

Too many dreams are killed before they ever get a chance to blossom because a person is an inappropriate support crew. A close friend or family member has the ability to crush a dream quicker than anyone else, simply because you love and trust them, when they may just be out of their element. That's why it's essential to be very deliberate when choosing who gets to be on your crew and on what subjects they get to have influence.

And while it's essential to have people support you in major decisions in your life, it's equally as important to give yourself permission to explore your ideas and dreams beyond someone else's opinion. Confidence doesn't come from being liked or loved; it comes from liking and loving yourself.

Here's what you can do to ensure you have the right people in your corner so when times get tough or when you're unsure about something, all you need to do is turn on the right "Bat Signal" and get ready for quality advice.

Make a list of the major areas of your life that are important to you. For most people it will look something like the chart below. For others, some categories will drop off and others will be added. Either use the list, below, or replicate the list with your categories.

List your current go-to people for advice in each category. Who do you actually ask for help when you need advice? You may find some people will fall into many categories. That's fine, especially at this stage. These lists are active. People are added and removed all the time, as we enter new seasons of life and our goals and desires evolve.

Think about who would be the ideal person for each category if you could have anyone in the world help you out.

ROLE	CURRENT	BEST FIT
Career/Business Advice		
Personal Advice		
Parenting Advice		
Health and Fitness Advice		
Wealth Creation Advice		
Relationship Advice		
Emotional Intelligence Advice		

If the person you wrote down in your best fit column is currently not aware you'd love to seek them out for help in these areas, let them know. If it's a family member or friend, you could say or write something like:

Hey, I want to let you know I really admire the way you [bring up your kids, run your business, handle your emotions, have an amazing relationship].

I am currently going through a transition in my life where I'm looking to improve in that area and I would like to ask you if I could reach out to you if I have any questions along the way. Would that be okay? I would really value and appreciate your advice.

Never be afraid to ask your friends for help, wisdom, or inspiration. That's what real friends are for.

And never be afraid to invest in finding the right mentors and coaches to help you. In the business world, this is often called "pay to play." Sometimes you can find great free information. I share a lot of information for free on my website and social channels. But you can get more personal attention and direction far faster by investing in hiring a coach or mentor to help you build the momentum you need to take massive action. Investing money in the process also motivates you to take action to achieve a return on your investment.

Over time, you'll find the right mentor or coach will not cost you anything in the long run. In fact, the right mentor or coach saves you time and makes you far more money than the amount of your investment. The most successful people in the world know this and invest regularly in mentors and coaches. Do what successful people do. Invest in your future.

Your Contribution

Support is a two-way street. The goal is not to put a team of people together to essentially work for you. All genuine people (like you) love to help and support people they care about. In order to create a support network that's mutually beneficial and bulletproof, you must also be a supporter and give generously to them.

Call, text, or email people in your life on a regular basis to let them know you're there for them and encourage them to reach out if there's anything you can do to help them. This is the true power of creating a support network. It's bigger than you. It's a collection of people all striving to live a life of meaning and purpose and to help others do the same.

In order for our network to grow stronger and more powerful, we must give our time, energy, and resources generously. We must make meaningful connections with new and old friends. Checking in and connecting with people on a regular basis is a core element of that. Over time, you'll both become integral parts of each other's success. Start today and take my Seven-Day Friends Challenge. Send a heartfelt message to one to three people in your network each day for the next seven days. Tell them one thing you appreciate about them and you're grateful for their friendship. Send a small gift to one or two people for no reason. It doesn't have to be big or expensive. I often send books to friends directly from Amazon. It takes two minutes, but builds massive good will. Try it. Send a book to a friend the next time you're in front of a computer.

An attendee at one of my recent events took this challenge and sent two small gifts to friends of hers. Each recipient cried tears of joy and said they had never been on the receiving end of something so simple, yet so meaningful. "The Seven-Day Friends Challenge," she told me, "is life changing." I'm confident you'll agree and continue for far longer than seven days. It's your turn. Start *Right Now*. Message someone to let them know one thing you appreciate about them and that you're grateful for them.

Developing a Supportive Community

I was fortunate to have learned this concept at an early age by playing as many team sports as would have me. In team sports, the entire team needed to work together as a unit to engineer a desired result.

The most powerful communities are the ones based off a common cause, common beliefs, and common values. In my health and fitness business we lead several communities of people who all work together to improve their health and fitness. One of them is a 17,000-member female-only community whose primary mission is to educate and motivate each other on how to live a healthy, active, and fulfilled life.

Supportive communities offer a sense of belonging and purpose. They also offer unique perspectives and diverse opinions and feedback. With the introduction of social media and, especially, Facebook and Facebook Groups, joining supportive communities has never been so easy. In fact, like information, these days, the issue is not finding a group, but choosing a group among the thousands and thousands of groups available.

Finding the Right Communities for You

The easiest way to find the right community for you is to go back to Phase 1. Grab that eulogy again, and find a group with a core purpose that's consistent with where you want to go. The clearer the mission of the community, the better the impact and effectiveness of the community will be for the members.

Finding groups with like-minded, positive, supportive people is critical. This is one place where the world's biggest giant, Facebook, can be used to your advantage. Search for groups with names that tell you the people in there share common goals and values. This way you'll know the people in there will know and understand what you're going through.

You could also join a group in an area where you're already doing well to surround yourself with like-minded people who can help you stay on track. That's the power of a community. You're not alone and have support. With the volume of in-person and virtual groups out there, there's a community out there waiting for you.

Once you're in, it's important that your membership provide a positive impact for both you and the others in the community. Here are five ways to do so.

1. Limit yourself to one or two communities at a time in each category of importance to you.

Don't spread yourself too thin. Facebook is an easy place to join way too many groups. Delete yourself from every group except your core few. This will be totally transformational, especially if you implement the next tip. It's good to have options, as that can allow you to not get locked into one way of thinking. But having too many options leads right back to information overload.

2. Provide as much value as you can.

Don't just enter a group with the mindset of "What can I get here?" or "Who can help me?" Enter with the mindset of "Who can I help and what can I provide?" The law of reciprocity is magnified in Facebook Groups. The more you give, the more you get out of it. In contrast, the people in the group who only speak up to ask for help rarely get much value in return. This is another reason why I suggest limiting yourself to a few communities. You simply can't give your all when you're spread too thin.

3. Commit a certain amount of time to each community each week.

If you're in a local community, it's great to physically meet up on a set schedule. Look at ways you can provide extra value and follow-up with the people in the community. A weekly text or video message to the community can go a long way. If it's an online group, schedule time to go and add value. Put it in your calendar and be there—be present—on a regular basis. Don't just wander in and out whenever you get the urge. You'll end up spending way too much time there and take away from your overall progress.

4. Build strong, authentic, and lasting relationships.

Some of my best relationships started from a community setting. The reason is natural. If you join a group because the members share similar goals and mindsets, you're essentially walking into a room with a bunch of people who enjoy what you enjoy. By adding value, it's natural that people will like you and you'll start to see powerful relationships form. You don't even need to look for the friendships. This process will happen naturally and they will automatically fall into place. Trust me on this one. As motivational speaker Zig Ziglar once said, "If you go looking for a friend, you're going to find they're scarce. If you go out to *be* a friend, you'll find them everywhere."

5. Become a super-connector.

What is a super-connector? A super-connector is someone who goes out of his or her way to identify win-win relationships and connect those people with no expectation of personal gain. A super-connector is assertive and doesn't just make introductions when asked, but rather initiates an introduction when they feel one would help the two people being introduced. A super-connector lets both people know how awesome the other one is and why he or she is making the introduction.

A super-connector oozes an abundant mindset. He or she fully believes that by connecting like-minded people he or she will create a massive positive impact on the lives of many people, including the people being introduced and the people in their circles of influence, and so on. Super-connectors provide the bridge and path to a better future for everyone.

I want you to become a super-connector. Doing so is easy. To start, list three pairs of people who you know would add value to each other in some way. These people may have similar interests, serve similar people, or share a similar experience. List those three pairs here and then reach out to each person individually. Tell each of them you'd like to introduce them to someone and you think it would be a great, mutually beneficial connection. Then tell them why. Once each of them agrees, make the introduction.

1.

2.

3.

Congratulations! You're now an official super-connector. Keep it up!

Automation and Technology (Your Friends or Foes?)

Superman has powers to either protect the Earth or destroy it. The same is true with the ever-increasing advancements in technology and automation. The smartphone is one of the greatest technological advancements ever created. You can talk, surf the web, play games, listen to music, watch video, pay for dinner, and so much more, directly from a gadget that fits in your pocket. It can also be your worst enemy.

Where is your phone? I bet it's within arm's reach, right? You see, we have allowed ourselves to become trapped in a world in which something has the power to help us advance, but in practice it becomes a distraction, and we're becoming worse off for it.

The next time you go out to dinner, before you take a seat, stop and take a look around the room. Look at who is on their phone? I was out to dinner a few nights ago and we walked past a table of eight young women, all around twenty years old. All of them were on their phones. I was amazed, although looking back I probably shouldn't have been. They were so interested in what was happening outside of the restaurant, none of them were present with the rest of their friends. They might as well have been sitting in different restaurants.

In this situation, their technology was a foe. Is this you? Are you on your phone when you're around others? As you know by now, even if my phone is near me, it's silent all day every day. I make sure I am off my phone around others and ask that they do the same when around me, even implementing a silent phone policy with out-of-town visitors.

That has created some awkward moments! When an old phone-addict friend came to stay with us for a few days, my rule increased the depth of the connections made under my roof and helped influence others to be more present in their homes. In fact, that same friend texted me to thank me for making him aware of his phone habits. He literally cut his phone usage in half since becoming aware of his addiction. Mission accomplished.

The key here is to use technology and automation to support positive outcomes in your life, free up your time and mind, and achieve your best life. Here are eight ways to use technology and automation to support positive outcomes on your path through the *Right Now* framework:

1. Using your phone to set frequent reminders that help you stay on track.

2. Using apps such as Evernote, Trello, and audio recorder to help document and organize your thoughts and ideas when you're on the run or capture great memories.

3. Set your phone to automatically switch to "do not disturb" mode when you're not using it or using Internet extensions to restrict Internet use to only certain preplanned times of

the day. Remain in control. Set an agenda and timetable and automatically open up technology only during your set times.

4. Detox from technology at least once a month. Schedule at least one full day to not look at your phone, computer, or TV screen.

5. Use technology to create rapid learning and advancements in knowledge. Think of technology and use it for good. Change your perception of its purpose. You have access to almost any information you want at the click of a button.

6. Use your global connection to reach and impact a global audience. Ten years ago I didn't know anyone who lived in the United States. Now I have dozens of very close friends from all over the world.

7. Automate nonessential, repeat services like bill payment, landscaping, and other services, so you can spend your time thinking about achieving your life goals and not worrying about scheduling oil delivery or when your credit card payment is due.

8. Outsource or automate everything but your top 10 percent. To do this, take a few minutes to write out all the things you do on a daily, weekly, monthly, or yearly basis. This could include things like exercise, doing the dishes, sending invoices, mowing the lawn, washing the car, bathing the kids, shower, etc. Out of that list, there will be about 5 to 10 percent only you can do. The rest can be done by others, often better than you. Circle the items that only you can do and then outsource or automate the rest. Outsourcing, even if it costs you money, often frees you up to take time to create more money by engaging in activities people will pay you for. More importantly, however, gearing up to do activities you don't enjoy or don't do well drains your energy and takes you away from activities that get you closer to your ideal life.

Do you feel empowered yet? You now have a big goal, a plan, and the skills and support to make it happen. The only thing that's left is for you to deliver. Don't worry, I'll help you do that next.

Now get ready to Deliver!

PHASE 4

DELIVER

CHAPTER 12

Your Rules for Life

In this final phase, the most exciting and worthwhile work begins. By this point you know exactly where you're going and how you're going to get there. All that's left to do is put the finishing touches on the plan and set you on your way to building your best life with great clarity and focus. Before I do, though, I want to share a little more information to help you move forward with even more impact.

It all starts with setting and enforcing your personal rules of life.

You know pretty well by now that I live a very deliberate life. To some, it may seem complicated to be so deliberate and intentional all day every day. In reality, however, it's actually simple, and it helps me control the outcomes of my actions beforehand, another valuable benefit.

A lot of people also think it sounds a bit crazy to be so focused. Yet again, the opposite is true. It's crazy *not* to live a deliberate life. It's crazy *not* to do everything you can to achieve everything you want.

At this point you know better than the people who doubt the value or simplicity with which you can live a deliberate and intentional life.

You also know how to use automation and technology to keep you focused without being enslaved.

What I am going to share next with you, however, is perhaps the best way I simplify and remain consistent in my life. This involves setting rules for my life that are both easy to remember and apply. The rules fall into two categories: Non-negotiables and Guidelines, which have a similar purpose, but vastly different responsibilities.

Non-negotiables are concrete rules you set for your life that are, you guessed it, not negotiable. They tell you what to do and when to do it. They happen no matter what. Here are four of my non-negotiables:

1. My phone is on silent 24/7. It's not negotiable. It's a must.
2. My alarms go off at regular intervals throughout the day to remind me of who I am and how I should be showing up. I don't care where I am. My alarms go off.
3. I tell my wife I love her every single day.
4. I provide value to my community daily.

There's no wiggle room with non-negotiables. I am deliberate and strict.

Non-negotiables give you confidence and resolve when faced with tough decisions. For example, a friend of mine doesn't borrow money. It's a non-negotiable. So every time he is in a store and the salesperson tries to sell him on the *great financing deal* they have with *zero interest for ninety days*, or even ninety years, he can confidently reply by saying "I don't borrow money. If you want to sell it to me you'll have to negotiate the price." In his case, he tells me his non-negotiable of not borrowing money has helped him confidently negotiate thousands of dollars off of sales prices for cash deals.

Guidelines are general principles to be aware of and live by. They are less concrete than non-negotiables, and the focus is on the policy or principle rather than a specific action or inaction. Three of my guidelines are:

1. I exercise a minimum of four times per week.
2. I eat a strict, healthy diet six days per week and allow some wiggle room on the seventh day for a treat.
3. I fly business class anytime I travel on a long flight.

I know the third one may sound snobbish to some people, but I have worked hard to put things in place to choose that luxury. Some people prefer to splurge on shoes, suits, or handbags. I can't stand sitting in a small plane seat for thirteen hours without being able to stretch or lie down.

Now it's your turn to create lists of non-negotiables and guidelines for your life. Start with two or three. As you get comfortable with it, do the exercise for all parts of your life, including health non-negotiables and guidelines, business non-negotiables and guidelines, relationship non-negotiables and guidelines, etc.

Here are some more examples of each to help you get started. If you're struggling to set non-negotiables start by trying some of these that you really connect with for a week and see how they feel. Then adjust as you go and become more aware of what's most important to you.

Non-negotiables
- I will never have my phone out when I am around others.
- I will write down ten things I'm grateful for when I wake up each morning and ten more before I go to sleep.
- I will read or listen to a book for at least sixty minutes each day.
- I will journal for at least fifteen minutes every day about my day, feelings, and anything else on my mind.
- I will have at least one date night with my spouse every week.

- I will reach out and add value to a friend at least once every week.
- I will pause to self-assess my day by asking myself how I performed and what I could do better tomorrow.
- I will do the 60x60x8 reset routine every day.
- I will do the 4x4 awareness of breath routine every day.
- I will film at least one free video training to help my community each week.
- I will provide massive value to my community every day.
- I will always say hello to others in elevators and anyone who comes within six feet of me.

Guidelines

- I will eat healthy every meal.
- I will meet with friends for a face-to-face catch ups as often as I can.
- I will reduce profanity.
- I will limit my coffee consumption.
- I will play golf at least two times each week.
- I will take at least five vacations each year.
- I will help connect like-minded friends.
- I will spend quality time with my family.

Take a few moments now and create your lists. You'll see I have also allocated columns for you to check. Is this a daily, weekly, monthly, or yearly item?

Item	Daily	Weekly	Monthly	Yearly
Non-negotiables				
Guidelines				

After a few days, come back to the list and assess how you're showing up. Are you following your non-negotiables and guidelines? If not, why not? Do you need to do some bad-habit breaking exercises? Assess yourself at least weekly after that as you incorporate these into your life.

After a while, most of these items on your list will happen on autopilot. Autopilot mode is reached when something becomes a habit and doesn't require much thinking. Just like tying your shoes, playing guitar, or typing on a keyboard without looking at your fingers are all byproducts of repetition and deliberate actions until the activity becomes thoughtless, living a life you truly desire is a byproduct of having meaningful non-negotiables and guidelines you repeat with deliberate actions over time until they are all on autopilot. With these in place, you're now ready for the final ingredients.

CHAPTER 13

The Roadblocks

B y now you've discovered and become aware of where you are in your life, where you want to go, how to get there, and how to move quickly and efficiently.

Right Now is the time to finalize your action plan and commit to the most important concepts of them all: the doing, the experiencing, the learning, and the growing.

Before we move onto the final thoughts, I'm going to help you avoid the thirteen most common roadblocks to your success. Look for these when you feel doubtful, stressed, or tired. Maybe one of these roadblocks is holding you back. Although we talk about some of these in more detail in previous chapters, I list them here to let you come back to this section when those feelings creep in to allow you to quickly identify what is holding you back.

1. Lack of desire

You'll only put the effort into something you truly desire. You must have a big enough reason to do the hard work. If you're feeling a lack of desire when working towards your life's purpose, ask yourself whether you truly want what you're chasing. Maybe you're having trouble identifying your true desire. Maybe you're still working towards a life you "should" live, rather than one you truly "want to" live.

2. The thoughts you feed your mind

If you have a thought that you aren't good enough or can't do something, does that give you a feeling of happiness or sadness? Does it make you feel powerful or less powerful? Think of something you can't do for a moment. How does it feel? How is your posture? Do you feel empowered to take action? Of course not.

Sometimes we put ourselves in the thought loop that something is too hard, or we can't do something, and then that causes us to stay in bed, or not make that call, or not do the hard work we need to do to succeed. That inaction reinforces the thought that whatever you're looking to accomplish is too hard or can't be done by you, and around and around you go.

Changing the thoughts you feed your mind will change your results.

3. You don't know where to start

Not knowing where to start is often more of an issue of having too much information than not enough. Because of that feeling, people get overwhelmed and do nothing. Because they do nothing, they get nothing and accomplish nothing.

To overcome this obstacle, ask someone who has had success doing what you want to do where you should start. Reach out in person, on the phone, on social media, or through email and ask. Start making connections with others who are doing what you want to do so you have people to support and who can support you. Share your successes, and if you get stuck again, ask for help again.

4. You already think you know

Some people think they already know what they need to know or they don't want to learn from someone who they perceive as being newer or younger. Being unwilling to learn from anyone and anything because you are a know-it-all is one of the toughest roadblocks to success. When you're a know-it-all, you block yourself from seeing invaluable lessons that are right in front of you that you need to learn in order to achieve true greatness.

5. Life is already okay

People in the business and personal development field, call this phenomenon "comfortable misery." You may be miserable, but you know the next paycheck will be deposited in two weeks and you are used to your boring routine. Boring days turn to boring weeks and months. Next thing you know, years have gone by and you're still barely scraping by because nothing kills motivation to do something different like comfort.

Generating enough income to put food on the table or live a comfortable life can hold you back from pursuing bigger dreams. Some people feel irresponsible moving away from that seemingly steady paycheck. Others won't take big action unless they are in pain or are forced to move. Are you stuck in a boring routine that's just okay?

6. Lack of support

We talked about support in more detail in previous chapters, so I won't go too deep into the different types of support you'll need to live a life of your dreams. I do want to emphasize, however, that a lack of support is almost always curable.

In order to have the right support you need to seek out individuals and groups that are relevant and experienced in what you're looking to accomplish. If you don't have the right support in your existing circle you'll feel stuck until you go out and find the support you need. Once you have the right people available to support you, it's also on you to tell them you're looking for support and what support you need. (In Chapter 11, I showed you several ways to find the support you need.)

7. Lack of action

Ideas are great. Dreams are important. Taking action is how ideas and dreams come to life. Make that phone call you know you should make. Go to the gym even when you're tired. Write the chapter of the book you want. Don't worry about being perfect. Don't worry about being wrong. Don't worry about making a small mistake, about being embarrassed, about what others might think. Make taking action your default response. Make taking action habitual. Otherwise, you'll be stuck with unfulfilled dreams.

8. You're not living consistent with your highest values

If you want to get fit and healthy, drinking beer and eating junk food will not get you there. If you want to have a better relationship, but you don't act lovingly, welcomingly, or openly, your relationship won't improve. If you're looking to increase sales, but you don't make the connections or the phone calls necessary to connect with more customers, you'll never achieve your sales goals. Once you establish your goals, it's critical that you act in a way that's consistent with what you're looking to achieve.

9. You think you need X before Y

Sometimes people run a script in their mind that they need to finish something before they can start something else, even if the two things are unrelated. Parents wait for their kids to graduate from college before leaving a job they hate to live a life of their dreams. Others have a savings goal they want to achieve before starting a home-based business. Still others wait for an event or to finish their college degree before pursuing their dreams.

Sometimes prerequisites are legitimate, such as going to medical school before becoming a doctor. Other times, the prerequisites are excuses, built on fear. Once one of those excuses is accomplished, another comes up. Success is always another "once I do this" away.

10. You're too busy saying "Yes" to everyone and everything

Are you too much of a "yes" man or woman? Do you say "yes" to other people so much that you have no time left for your own dreams? This is a big roadblock for mothers, especially, who spend decades putting other people ahead of their own dreams.

Saying "yes" to too many things will leave you tired and unsatisfied. Before saying "yes" to anything else I want you to make sure the answers to each of these six questions reinforce the decision to say yes. If not, politely say "no" and redirect the time you'd have spent doing that activity towards building the life of your dreams:

a. Do I want to get involved?
b. What is the purpose of this?
c. What difference will this make in my life now and in the long term?
d. What will I have to give up if I say yes to this? What will I have to say no to?
e. What is the ideal outcome of this activity?
f. Can I be 100 percent engaged in this activity?

If you want to get involved, believe in the purpose, see a desirable short and long-term purpose, won't lose focus on anything more important, desire the ideal outcome of the activity, and can be 100 percent engaged, then it's a yes. If not, it's a no.

11. You're not taking personal responsibility

It's no one else's responsibility for you to succeed in any area of your life but your own. Yes there are times when you rely on someone who doesn't come through, but in every instance there's something you can do to continue to build momentum towards your goal. If your workout partner is sick, that doesn't mean you can skip the gym if you want to get in better shape. If your business partner doesn't make enough sales calls, that doesn't mean you can't or shouldn't make more yourself. Looking for blame or an excuse will keep you from doing what you need to do to make your dreams come true. Take personal responsibility for achieving your goals.

12. Procrastination

Procrastination is more than just a productivity killer. Studies show procrastination causes physiological reactions that can make you gain weight and stress to the point of a heart attack. It's literally a silent killer. Yet so many people are chronic procrastinators, waiting for the perfect time to work on something or until something is perfect to release it to the world.

The truth is there will never be a perfect time to work on a project. You'll have aches, pains, commitments, and more. The results you achieve will never be perfect either. Procrastination will stop you from achieving your goals. It will affect the people around you. And it will affect the people who need the benefit of your work. Your procrastination is holding those people back by keeping your projects from them.

To eliminate procrastination, set a specific goal and ask yourself or your peers if it's achievable within a certain time frame. Once you get informed and set a goal, ask your peers to hold you accountable. Ask the support group you develop in Chapter 11 to keep you accountable. Announce your goal on social media. Attach consequences. Work in small blocks of uninterrupted time. Build the willpower muscle.

Like almost anything, eliminating procrastination will take time and effort, but the effort will be worth it. What would happen if you started earlier—*Right Now*—on building a life of your dreams? Who would benefit from your work?

13. Fear

Fear can keep you from taking the actions necessary to accomplish your goals. Fear can be debilitating and comes in many forms. People fear many things, such as poverty, criticism, ill health, early death, loss of love, old age, and even success.

In order to keep fear from sabotaging your success, it's important to understand most fear isn't real. Fear is a state of mind. It's a protection mechanism that must exist in many parts of life. Fear tells us not to touch a hot stove or jump in a lion's cage at the zoo. Fear must exist for us to survive, but only when it's based in reality.

As President Franklin D. Roosevelt famously said, "The only thing we have to fear is fear itself."

With life and business building, however, the fear that holds people back is not based in reality, but in our imaginations. People think of the worst case scenarios no matter how unlikely they may be and then allow that fear to freeze them. They fear all the negative consequences but fail to consider the many positive, and often more likely, outcomes.

Did any of these obstacles feel familiar? Many people find a few of these have been big obstacles on a regular basis. That's okay. You know to look for them now, exactly what they are, and that they are holding you back from achieving the success you want. By identifying them and following the rest of the steps in this process you'll be able to push past them because you know something much, much better is waiting for you on the other side of those obstacles. None of the time we have spent together will mean anything to you if you do not take action based on the lessons and principles I have shared with you.

One of the most popular movie series when I was growing up was called *Rocky*. The movie is about a small-time boxer from Philadelphia, Pennsylvania, named Rocky Balboa, who gets a chance to fight the heavy-weight champion of the world. As you might imagine, Rocky is a big underdog. He is also uneducated, but street smart, with a tenacious will. It's a great movie, so rent it if you haven't seen it! I was super inspired by several parts of the movie, especially this great quote from Rocky:

> Let me tell you something you already know. The world ain't all sunshine and rainbows. It's a very mean and nasty place, and I don't care how tough you are, it will beat you to your knees and keep you there permanently if you let it. You, me, or nobody is gonna hit as hard as life. But it ain't about how hard you hit. It's about how hard you can get hit and keep moving forward; how much you can take and keep moving forward. That's how winning is done! Now, if you know what you're worth, then go out and get what you're worth. But you gotta be willing to take the hits, and not point fingers saying you ain't where you wanna be because of him, or her, or anybody. Cowards do that and that ain't you. You're better than that!

There's a lot of wisdom in that statement. Keep it close to you.

And remember, there's nothing that can ever stop you from living the life you truly desire if you follow this process.

Four Points to Keep Close as You Get Started

1. Design your vision and desired outcome.
Intention and direction are powerful. If you're aiming at something truly meaningful to you there's no stopping you.

2. Embrace the struggle.

Accept that fear and struggle are going to happen. There's no avoiding it. When you acknowledge this up front you'll be ready for whatever comes at you. Adapting this mindset allows you to mentally prepare in ways that produce extraordinary results.

3. Know the start is always the hardest.

It's a fact. When you were learning how to walk, tie your shoelaces, drive a car, or kiss someone, it was hard, awkward, or both. Don't expect anything different when you're attempting something new like what you've learned here. It's a rule of life. Know the more time and energy you put into the *Right Now* framework, the easier it will become, and the more value you'll create for yourself and others. Expect it to be hard at first.

4. Find hope from the Chinese Bamboo Tree.

The Chinese Bamboo Tree is unlike most others. When you plant it you don't see anything happen for quite a while. In fact, it can stay underground for up to four years. That's right, you can spend four years watering a patch of dirt and not see anything happen.

At some point, however, the Chinese Bamboo Tree bursts out of the ground with gusto. In just five weeks, after up to four years of hiding underground, the Chinese Bamboo Tree can reach its full size. By full size, I am not talking about some puny tree you can keep on your desk. I'm not talking about some bush either. I'm not even talking about your standard apple tree or even a run-of-the-mill pine. Within five weeks, a Chinese Bamboo Tree can grow up to ninety feet tall! (That's not a typo.)

Your journey to achieving your true purpose in life can take a similar path. You can spend months working hard, doing all the right things, and still not *see* the growth you want. But if you're doing all the right things, it's happening. You might even have moments where you start questioning your sanity. But keep on track. If you're following a well-thought-out plan, it's only a matter of time before you break through the ground and blossom high into the sky.

Keep at it. Be the Chinese Bamboo Tree. Keep watering that dirt. Keep assessing, adjusting, and believing in yourself, your vision, and your plan. You, too, will bust through the dirt and launch high into the sky before you know it.

Hold Yourself Accountable

As a reminder to yourself of all the good you have in you, here's what I want you to do: Write a letter to yourself.

Take a sheet of paper. At the top write today's date. Skip a line and write "Dear" and then your first name. Then write a letter to yourself about your intentions and the things you'll achieve over the next ninety days.

When you're done, fold up the letter and put it somewhere. Set a reminder in your phone for ninety days from now to read the letter. Be sure to include where you put the letter, so you can find it right away!

Ninety days from now one of two things will happen. You'll have either done nothing and spent ninety days helping someone else live their dream at the expense of your own. Or you'll have spent ninety days building momentum towards living *your* dream life, likely far exceeding your expectations listed in the letter.

Final Thoughts: Why not *you* and why not *now*?

As you look back on your life, I want you to be able to honestly say you lived with intention, loved with passion, and never gave up on your dreams. I want, when your family and friends gather to say their final goodbyes, for the eulogy they all hear to be the same one you wrote in Phase 1, because that's the life you created for yourself.

The path will not be a straight line. It will have ups and downs. It will zig and it will zag. But you have all the tools at your disposal to build a life of true purpose.

You've just completed a process in which you discovered your true purpose in life, designed your schedule and surroundings to support your new path, began developing yourself and your support to help continue towards personal fulfillment, and, finally, started delivering the best results possible.

You have a system designed to be flexible and customizable because there's *no* one-size-fits-all life. But there's *your* life. And you have *your* plan. You have a plan you can customize to adapt it to your unique challenges and opportunities. No matter where you are or what you face, you can do *something*, *Right Now*, to start building momentum towards your ideal life. Your steps may be small, or they may be large. But you're ready to take *some* steps towards a life that matters.

I have challenged you to think and act outside of your comfort zone. And I will continue to be here for you. My contact information and additional resources are waiting for you on the resources page at http://brettcampbell.net/right-now-resources

It's your time to do *something* to start building momentum, *Right Now*, towards living your ideal life. Don't wait for a tragedy, like I did, to realize you haven't been living a life true to your larger purpose. Find your motivation, *Right Now*, and then take action, because there's no reason you can't start building momentum towards achieving your biggest dreams.

The choice is yours.

You *are* worthy. And you *are* ready.

So why not *you*? And why not *now*?

Right Now!

An Unexpected Case Study

I am a full-time writer. (I've waited a long time to be able to say that!)

In fact, nowadays not only do I write for myself, but I also help other people write their books (and communicate their messages), to make sure they are clearly and easily understood. I choose my projects carefully, working only with people I believe in and who also have messages I believe can impact people in a positive way.

So when Brett reached out to me with a manuscript he said contained a process for "discovering your true purpose" and "building momentum towards living your ideal life," I was intrigued, but I have to admit I was also a bit skeptical. I've read too many so-called "authors" who've read a few books, added an acronym or two, and then promoted the recycled material as a "system" for accomplishing goals faster or better.

That said, when I first read Brett's draft of *Right Now* I was pleasantly surprised to find it refreshing; Brett was both transparent and authentic in how he had faced certain challenges in his life.

And although several parts of Brett's system seemed intuitive or were known to me from reading countless self-help, business, and parenting books, other parts (or the application of his ideas) were new to me. Brett's personal story set him apart from many of the others, even putting familiar concepts in a different light. I found Brett to be confident, yet casual and relatable.

But the most impressive thing for me: Brett is "self-made."

He came from turmoil and built stability with intention. He wasn't handed the keys to the castle, he built it, one brick at a time. Brett worked, and he worked hard and smart.

That sets Brett apart.

But, quite honestly, I still wasn't sure how much it would resonate with me personally. I was working full-time in a professional "day job" and working nights and weekends working on my own writing and freelance writing. Yes, I had a goal: my desire was to be a full-time writer—but I had a family to support, and even though it had been a goal for years, most days it felt like an impossibility.

But as I began to work with Brett on *Right Now*, I started to experiment with several parts of Brett's system.

I ordered a full-year, laminated wall calendar and for the first time I scheduled my year with more vacation, family, and rest days than ever. (But the shocking part was I actually *took* days off, not just scheduled them!)

I adopted the mindset of asking "opposite" questions; writing and living the eulogy I would want my relatives to be able to read honestly at my funeral.

I wrote down several non-negotiables and guidelines and began to hold myself accountable to actually stick to them. (And saying "no" to things turned out to actually be freeing.)

I started moving more, taking the stairs for anything under five floors. And since Brett recommends drinking tons more water (which I knew was a good idea but never did), I decided I could get the benefits of doing both: so even though I work on the fourth floor, I made a commitment to drink more water and use the restroom on the first floor! It seems simple but going up and down four flights of stairs several times a day has been really good for me. It only takes a minute longer to use the stairs, but it gets me some much needed exercise and actually has put me in a more powerful mindset for work.

I even started outsourcing several areas of my life where I wasn't using my time wisely. I hired a virtual assistant to take over tasks I *could* do, and would normally do myself, leaving me more time to do the tasks that I'm best at.

But the most surprising thing for me was something I hadn't planned on. By the time I was finishing up working with Brett on *Right Now*, I had actually flipped from working full-time in my profession to *working full-time writing* and working part-time in my profession—I had reached a goal I often felt wasn't attainable.

Coincidence? I think not.

With my change to writing full-time, I can now schedule my time around what's most important to me and that starts with a daily walk with my two kids before school. We simply spend time together exploring our neighborhood and talking about the sights, sounds, and animals, and getting some much needed fresh air before they have to go school. Surprisingly, my kids went from wailing "Don't make me get up, I'm too tired!" at 7:30 a.m. to hopping out of bed at 6:30 a.m. like it's Christmas morning to go for "our walk."

In fact, our neighbors began noticing, too, asking me about the walks and then starting to take walks themselves. In just a few weeks, we are up to three of the seven families on our street going for regular family walks!

The bottom line is by the time the book was done I was healthier, stronger, and had more energy. My writing business was accelerating.

But most important of all, my family was happier than we had been in years.

Yes, I *could have* done all that before working with Brett on his book.

But the reality is that I didn't.

Implementing Brett's framework for creating my ideal life wasn't something I planned on doing when I started out working on *Right Now*.

But the core of his message, *Why not you? Why not now?* unexpectedly hit home with me.

And I'm very grateful it did.

Nick Pavlidis
Writer and Content Coach
NickPavlidis.com

Resources

WAIT! We haven't finished yet.

Your journey has only just begun. And of course, I'll never leave you hanging – remember, we're in this together!

Over the past few years I've discovered, developed, or created resources specifically designed to help you get the fastest impact in achieving what you *truly* want in your life. I've set up a "one-stop" place for you to find many of these *free* resources ranging from workshops, seminars, radio shows, podcasts, videos, and more, at <u>http://brettcampbell.net/right-now-resources</u>.

In addition to those, I've developed two other resources to help you master the *Right Now* framework and take your life and business to the next level: *Unleash Your Greatness* and the *Authority Academy*, which both provide you additional opportunities to learn and engage with me and others who are looking to improve their personal, business, or professional lives.

In *Unleash Your Greatness*, I walk you through the *Right Now* framework, answer your personal questions, help you bust through common obstacles, and make sure nothing is holding you back from taking massive action.

In *Authority Academy*, I help you turn your passion, skills, and knowledge into newfound profits that can support your new direction. It's where I coach Internet marketers, speakers, other coaches, and small business owners on how to find the right customers, build their customer base, and make more money. I provide swipe files, templates, and exclusive content, all designed to help you take major action *immediately*. It's an opportunity, from wherever you are, to connect with me, and others, who are challenging themselves to take things to the next level.

You can find more information about *Unleash Your Greatness* and *Authority Academy* on the resources page, too: http://brettcampbell.net/right-now-resources.

Also, please check out my speaking schedule (and booking opportunities) at: http://brettcampbell.net/speaking.

One more thing!

I would love to have more ways to engage with you and help you achieve your goals and dreams! Join the *Right Now* Community with me on Facebook: http://brettcampbell.net/rightnow. The Facebook Community is where I can share the latest applications and newest content with you, including videos, livestreams, blogs, podcasts, and more.

Last, but not least, I'd love to hear from you directly!

Send me a message about how *Right Now* has impacted you. My personal address is brett@brettcampbell.net. Your message will come right to me and I give you my word, I read each, and every, email.

I look forward to hearing from you and learning what you are doing *Right Now* to live your truest and best life!

About the Author

 Brett Campbell is the owner and CEO of *Fit International*, a global health and fitness company whose products and services have helped over 45,000 clients, and the *Authority Academy*, an online community for Internet marketers, coaches, speakers, and small business owners. He is also the founder of the *Unleash Your Greatness* movement, an international live-event series to help others pursue living the life of their dreams. Brett's messages reach over five million people each week.

Having grown up in New Zealand, Brett lives in his dream house on the beach of the Gold Coast of Australia with his lovely wife, Emily, and their two Pugs, Burt and Puggsly.

Morgan James makes all of our titles available
through the Library for All Charity Organizations.

www.LibraryForAll.org